Policy Management Tools
Complete Self-Assessment Guide

C000150969

The guidance in this Self-Assessment is based
Tools best practices and standards in business process architecture,
design and quality management. The guidance is also based on the
professional judgment of the individual collaborators listed in the
Acknowledgments.

Notice of rights

You are licensed to use the Self-Assessment contents in your presentations and materials for internal use and customers without asking us - we are here to help.

All rights reserved for the book itself: this book may not be reproduced or transmitted in any form by any means, electronic, mechanical, photocopying, recording, or otherwise, without the prior written permission of the publisher.

The information in this book is distributed on an "As Is" basis without warranty. While every precaution has been taken in the preparation of he book, neither the author nor the publisher shall have any liability to any person or entity with respect to any loss or damage caused or alleged to be caused directly or indirectly by the instructions contained in this book or by the products described in it.

Trademarks

Many of the designations used by manufacturers and sellers to distinguish their products are claimed as trademarks. Where those designations appear in this book, and the publisher was aware of a trademark claim, the designations appear as requested by the owner of the trademark. All other product names and services identified throughout this book are used in editorial fashion only and for the benefit of such companies with no intention of infringement of the trademark. No such use, or the use of any trade name, is intended to convey endorsement or other affiliation with this book.

Copyright © by The Art of Service
http://theartofservice.com
service@theartofservice.com

Table of Contents

About The Art of Service

The Art of Service, Business Process Architects since 2000, is dedicated to helping stakeholders achieve excellence.

Defining, designing, creating, and implementing a process to solve a stakeholders challenge or meet an objective is the most valuable role… In EVERY group, company, organization and department.

Unless you're talking a one-time, single-use project, there should be a process. Whether that process is managed and implemented by humans, AI, or a combination of the two, it needs to be designed by someone with a complex enough perspective to ask the right questions.

Someone capable of asking the right questions and step back and say, 'What are we really trying to accomplish here? And is there a different way to look at it?'

With The Art of Service's Standard Requirements Self-Assessments, we empower people who can do just that — whether their title is marketer, entrepreneur, manager, salesperson, consultant, Business Process Manager, executive assistant, IT Manager, CIO etc... —they are the people who rule the future. They are people who watch the process as it happens, and ask the right questions to make the process work better.

Contact us when you need any support with this Self-Assessment and any help with templates, blue-prints and examples of standard documents you might need:

http://theartofservice.com
service@theartofservice.com

Included Resources - how to access

Included with your purchase of the book is the Policy

Management Tools Self-Assessment Spreadsheet Dashboard which contains all questions and Self-Assessment areas and auto-generates insights, graphs, and project RACI planning - all with examples to get you started right away.

How? Simply send an email to
access@theartofservice.com
with this books' title in the subject to get the Policy Management Tools Self Assessment Tool right away.

You will receive the following contents with New and Updated specific criteria:

- The latest quick edition of the book in PDF

- The latest complete edition of the book in PDF, which criteria correspond to the criteria in...

- The Self-Assessment Excel Dashboard, and...

- Example pre-filled Self-Assessment Excel Dashboard to get familiar with results generation

- In-depth specific Checklists covering the topic

- Project management checklists and templates to assist with implementation

INCLUDES LIFETIME SELF ASSESSMENT UPDATES

Every self assessment comes with Lifetime Updates and Lifetime Free Updated Books. Lifetime Updates is an industry-first feature which allows you to receive verified self assessment updates, ensuring you always have the most accurate information at your fingertips.

Get it now- you will be glad you did - do it now, before you forget.

Send an email to **access@theartofservice.com** with this books' title in the subject to get the Policy Management Tools Self Assessment Tool right away.

Purpose of this Self-Assessment

This Self-Assessment has been developed to improve understanding of the requirements and elements of Policy Management Tools, based on best practices and standards in business process architecture, design and quality management.

It is designed to allow for a rapid Self-Assessment to determine how closely existing management practices and procedures correspond to the elements of the Self-Assessment.

The criteria of requirements and elements of Policy Management Tools have been rephrased in the format of a Self-Assessment questionnaire, with a seven-criterion scoring system, as explained in this document.

In this format, even with limited background knowledge of Policy Management Tools, a manager can quickly review existing operations to determine how they measure up to the standards. This in turn can serve as the starting point of a 'gap analysis' to identify management tools or system elements that might usefully be implemented in the organization to help improve overall performance.

How to use the Self-Assessment

On the following pages are a series of questions to identify to what extent your Policy Management Tools initiative is complete in comparison to the requirements set in standards.

To facilitate answering the questions, there is a space in front of each question to enter a score on a scale of '1' to '5'.

1 Strongly Disagree

2 Disagree

3 Neutral

4 Agree

5 Strongly Agree

Read the question and rate it with the following in front of mind:

'In my belief, the answer to this question is clearly defined'.

There are two ways in which you can choose to interpret this statement;
1. how aware are you that the answer to the question is clearly defined
2. for more in-depth analysis you can choose to gather evidence and confirm the answer to the question. This obviously will take more time, most Self-Assessment users opt for the first way to interpret the question and dig deeper later on based on the outcome of the overall Self-Assessment.

A score of '1' would mean that the answer is not clear at all, where a '5' would mean the answer is crystal clear and defined. Leave emtpy when the question is not applicable or you don't want to answer it, you can skip it without affecting your score. Write your score in the space provided.

After you have responded to all the appropriate statements in each section, compute your average score for that section, using the formula provided, and round to the nearest tenth. Then transfer to the corresponding spoke in the Policy Management Tools Scorecard on the second next page of the Self-Assessment.

Your completed Policy Management Tools Scorecard will give you a clear presentation of which Policy Management Tools areas need attention.

Policy Management Tools
Scorecard Example

Example of how the finalized Scorecard can look like:

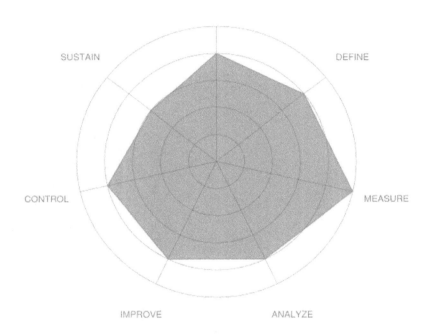

Policy Management Tools Scorecard

Your Scores:

BEGINNING OF THE SELF-ASSESSMENT:

CRITERION #1: RECOGNIZE

INTENT: Be aware of the need for change. Recognize that there is an unfavorable variation, problem or symptom.

In my belief, the answer to this question is clearly defined:

5 Strongly Agree

4 Agree

3 Neutral

2 Disagree

1 Strongly Disagree

1. Are there recognized policy management tools problems?
<--- Score

2. Do you recognize policy management tools achievements?
<--- Score

3. Who should resolve the policy management tools

issues?
<--- Score

4. Where is training needed?
<--- Score

5. Why is this needed?
<--- Score

6. Which issues are too important to ignore?
<--- Score

7. Would you recognize a threat from the inside?
<--- Score

8. What does policy management tools success mean to the stakeholders?
<--- Score

9. How do you recognize an policy management tools objection?
<--- Score

10. Will it solve real problems?
<--- Score

11. What do you need to start doing?
<--- Score

12. What activities does the governance board need to consider?
<--- Score

13. What is the extent or complexity of the policy management tools problem?
<--- Score

14. Why the need?
<--- Score

15. What policy management tools events should you attend?
<--- Score

16. Can management personnel recognize the monetary benefit of policy management tools?
<--- Score

17. Do you need to avoid or amend any policy management tools activities?
<--- Score

18. How do you identify subcontractor relationships?
<--- Score

19. Are problem definition and motivation clearly presented?
<--- Score

20. Is the need for organizational change recognized?
<--- Score

21. To what extent does each concerned units management team recognize policy management tools as an effective investment?
<--- Score

22. Which information does the policy management tools business case need to include?
<--- Score

23. Are employees recognized for desired behaviors?

<--- Score

24. For your policy management tools project, identify and describe the business environment, is there more than one layer to the business environment?
<--- Score

25. Is it needed?
<--- Score

26. What policy management tools capabilities do you need?
<--- Score

27. What is the smallest subset of the problem you can usefully solve?
<--- Score

28. Are you dealing with any of the same issues today as yesterday? What can you do about this?
<--- Score

29. What would happen if policy management tools weren't done?
<--- Score

30. How do you identify the kinds of information that you will need?
<--- Score

31. What are your needs in relation to policy management tools skills, labor, equipment, and markets?
<--- Score

32. Who needs budgets?

<--- Score

33. When a policy management tools manager recognizes a problem, what options are available?
<--- Score

34. Who needs to know?
<--- Score

35. Is it clear when you think of the day ahead of you what activities and tasks you need to complete?
<--- Score

36. What needs to stay?
<--- Score

37. What prevents you from making the changes you know will make you a more effective policy management tools leader?
<--- Score

38. What are the minority interests and what amount of minority interests can be recognized?
<--- Score

39. What are the clients issues and concerns?
<--- Score

40. Where do you need to exercise leadership?
<--- Score

41. How are you going to measure success?
<--- Score

42. Whom do you really need or want to serve?
<--- Score

43. Is the quality assurance team identified?
<--- Score

44. What information do users need?
<--- Score

45. How are the policy management tools's objectives aligned to the group's overall stakeholder strategy?
<--- Score

46. Who defines the rules in relation to any given issue?
<--- Score

47. Are there regulatory / compliance issues?
<--- Score

48. What else needs to be measured?
<--- Score

49. As a sponsor, customer or management, how important is it to meet goals, objectives?
<--- Score

50. What training and capacity building actions are needed to implement proposed reforms?
<--- Score

51. Are there any specific expectations or concerns about the policy management tools team, policy management tools itself?
<--- Score

52. What are the timeframes required to resolve each of the issues/problems?

<--- Score

53. What is the problem and/or vulnerability?
<--- Score

54. How do you take a forward-looking perspective in identifying policy management tools research related to market response and models?
<--- Score

55. Looking at each person individually – does every one have the qualities which are needed to work in this group?
<--- Score

56. What are the policy management tools resources needed?
<--- Score

57. What are the expected benefits of policy management tools to the stakeholder?
<--- Score

58. What creative shifts do you need to take?
<--- Score

59. How does it fit into your organizational needs and tasks?
<--- Score

60. Will policy management tools deliverables need to be tested and, if so, by whom?
<--- Score

61. What are the stakeholder objectives to be achieved with policy management tools?

<--- Score

62. What is the problem or issue?
<--- Score

63. What resources or support might you need?
<--- Score

64. How can auditing be a preventative security measure?
<--- Score

65. Did you miss any major policy management tools issues?
<--- Score

66. How are training requirements identified?
<--- Score

67. Do you know what you need to know about policy management tools?
<--- Score

68. What needs to be done?
<--- Score

69. What problems are you facing and how do you consider policy management tools will circumvent those obstacles?
<--- Score

70. Are there any revenue recognition issues?
<--- Score

71. Are controls defined to recognize and contain problems?

<--- Score

72. Who else hopes to benefit from it?
<--- Score

73. Have you identified your policy management tools key performance indicators?
<--- Score

74. Consider your own policy management tools project, what types of organizational problems do you think might be causing or affecting your problem, based on the work done so far?
<--- Score

75. Will new equipment/products be required to facilitate policy management tools delivery, for example is new software needed?
<--- Score

76. What should be considered when identifying available resources, constraints, and deadlines?
<--- Score

77. To what extent would your organization benefit from being recognized as a award recipient?
<--- Score

78. Are employees recognized or rewarded for performance that demonstrates the highest levels of integrity?
<--- Score

79. Do you need different information or graphics?
<--- Score

80. What policy management tools coordination do you need?
<--- Score

81. Do you have/need 24-hour access to key personnel?
<--- Score

82. Who are your key stakeholders who need to sign off?
<--- Score

83. How much are sponsors, customers, partners, stakeholders involved in policy management tools? In other words, what are the risks, if policy management tools does not deliver successfully?
<--- Score

84. Does the problem have ethical dimensions?
<--- Score

85. Are your goals realistic? Do you need to redefine your problem? Perhaps the problem has changed or maybe you have reached your goal and need to set a new one?
<--- Score

86. Will a response program recognize when a crisis occurs and provide some level of response?
<--- Score

87. What situation(s) led to this policy management tools Self Assessment?
<--- Score

88. Does policy management tools create potential

expectations in other areas that need to be recognized and considered?
<--- Score

89. How do you assess your policy management tools workforce capability and capacity needs, including skills, competencies, and staffing levels?
<--- Score

90. Who needs what information?
<--- Score

91. What vendors make products that address the policy management tools needs?
<--- Score

92. What do employees need in the short term?
<--- Score

93. Think about the people you identified for your policy management tools project and the project responsibilities you would assign to them, what kind of training do you think they would need to perform these responsibilities effectively?
<--- Score

94. What tools and technologies are needed for a custom policy management tools project?
<--- Score

95. How many trainings, in total, are needed?
<--- Score

96. How do you recognize an objection?
<--- Score

Add up total points for this section:
_____ = Total points for this section

Divided by: _____ (number of
statements answered) = _____
Average score for this section

Transfer your score to the policy
management tools Index at the
beginning of the Self-Assessment.

CRITERION #2: DEFINE:

INTENT: Formulate the stakeholder problem. Define the problem, needs and objectives.

In my belief, the answer to this question is clearly defined:

5 Strongly Agree

4 Agree

3 Neutral

2 Disagree

1 Strongly Disagree

1. Are there any constraints known that bear on the ability to perform policy management tools work? How is the team addressing them?
<--- Score

2. What are the record-keeping requirements of policy management tools activities?
<--- Score

3. What are the requirements for audit information?
<--- Score

4. Is there a completed SIPOC representation, describing the Suppliers, Inputs, Process, Outputs, and Customers?
<--- Score

5. Are audit criteria, scope, frequency and methods defined?
<--- Score

6. Are the policy management tools requirements complete?
<--- Score

7. Is there a policy management tools management charter, including stakeholder case, problem and goal statements, scope, milestones, roles and responsibilities, communication plan?
<--- Score

8. Is the team adequately staffed with the desired cross-functionality? If not, what additional resources are available to the team?
<--- Score

9. How is the team tracking and documenting its work?
<--- Score

10. Has anyone else (internal or external to the group) attempted to solve this problem or a similar one before? If so, what knowledge can be leveraged from these previous efforts?
<--- Score

11. Why are you doing policy management tools and what is the scope?
<--- Score

12. Is policy management tools currently on schedule according to the plan?
<--- Score

13. When is the estimated completion date?
<--- Score

14. How and when will the baselines be defined?
<--- Score

15. Is data collected and displayed to better understand customer(s) critical needs and requirements.
<--- Score

16. Are customer(s) identified and segmented according to their different needs and requirements?
<--- Score

17. What information should you gather?
<--- Score

18. How would you define the culture at your organization, how susceptible is it to policy management tools changes?
<--- Score

19. What are the core elements of the policy management tools business case?
<--- Score

20. Who is gathering information?
<--- Score

21. What constraints exist that might impact the team?
<--- Score

22. How do you keep key subject matter experts in the loop?
<--- Score

23. Are there different segments of customers?
<--- Score

24. Have all of the relationships been defined properly?
<--- Score

25. Is it clearly defined in and to your organization what you do?
<--- Score

26. When is/was the policy management tools start date?
<--- Score

27. Has a project plan, Gantt chart, or similar been developed/completed?
<--- Score

28. Is the current 'as is' process being followed? If not, what are the discrepancies?
<--- Score

29. Are all requirements met?
<--- Score

30. When are meeting minutes sent out? Who is on the distribution list?
<--- Score

31. Is there a critical path to deliver policy management tools results?
<--- Score

32. What are the dynamics of the communication plan?
<--- Score

33. Are roles and responsibilities formally defined?
<--- Score

34. Are required metrics defined, what are they?
<--- Score

35. How will the policy management tools team and the group measure complete success of policy management tools?
<--- Score

36. Do you have a policy management tools success story or case study ready to tell and share?
<--- Score

37. Have specific policy objectives been defined?
<--- Score

38. Is the improvement team aware of the different versions of a process: what they think it is vs. what it actually is vs. what it should be vs. what it could be?
<--- Score

39. What is the scope of the policy management tools effort?
<--- Score

40. How do you gather policy management tools requirements?
<--- Score

41. How do you gather the stories?
<--- Score

42. What is in scope?
<--- Score

43. Has the improvement team collected the 'voice of the customer' (obtained feedback – qualitative and quantitative)?
<--- Score

44. Are accountability and ownership for policy management tools clearly defined?
<--- Score

45. What is a worst-case scenario for losses?
<--- Score

46. Are the policy management tools requirements testable?
<--- Score

47. Where can you gather more information?
<--- Score

48. How do you manage scope?
<--- Score

49. Who are the policy management tools improvement team members, including Management Leads and Coaches?
<--- Score

50. How do you gather requirements?
<--- Score

51. What happens if policy management tools's scope changes?
<--- Score

52. What baselines are required to be defined and managed?
<--- Score

53. How do you catch policy management tools definition inconsistencies?
<--- Score

54. What is out-of-scope initially?
<--- Score

55. What are the rough order estimates on cost savings/opportunities that policy management tools brings?
<--- Score

56. How was the 'as is' process map developed, reviewed, verified and validated?
<--- Score

57. Is the policy management tools scope complete and appropriately sized?
<--- Score

58. Is scope creep really all bad news?
<--- Score

59. How do you manage changes in policy management tools requirements?
<--- Score

60. What are the compelling stakeholder reasons for embarking on policy management tools?
<--- Score

61. What key stakeholder process output measure(s) does policy management tools leverage and how?
<--- Score

62. What sort of initial information to gather?
<--- Score

63. Is the policy management tools scope manageable?
<--- Score

64. What is the definition of policy management tools excellence?
<--- Score

65. What is in the scope and what is not in scope?
<--- Score

66. What are the tasks and definitions?
<--- Score

67. What scope do you want your strategy to cover?
<--- Score

68. What are (control) requirements for policy management tools Information?
<--- Score

69. Scope of sensitive information?
<--- Score

70. How do you build the right business case?
<--- Score

71. What is the context?
<--- Score

72. How do you manage unclear policy management tools requirements?
<--- Score

73. Has/have the customer(s) been identified?
<--- Score

74. How do you hand over policy management tools context?
<--- Score

75. How did the policy management tools manager receive input to the development of a policy management tools improvement plan and the estimated completion dates/times of each activity?
<--- Score

76. Have the customer needs been translated into specific, measurable requirements? How?
<--- Score

77. Is there any additional policy management tools definition of success?

<--- Score

78. What system do you use for gathering policy management tools information?
<--- Score

79. What defines best in class?
<--- Score

80. Is policy management tools required?
<--- Score

81. Does the team have regular meetings?
<--- Score

82. Has the policy management tools work been fairly and/or equitably divided and delegated among team members who are qualified and capable to perform the work? Has everyone contributed?
<--- Score

83. Will team members regularly document their policy management tools work?
<--- Score

84. Who approved the policy management tools scope?
<--- Score

85. If substitutes have been appointed, have they been briefed on the policy management tools goals and received regular communications as to the progress to date?
<--- Score

86. Are resources adequate for the scope?

<--- Score

87. How have you defined all policy management tools requirements first?
<--- Score

88. How do you think the partners involved in policy management tools would have defined success?
<--- Score

89. What policy management tools requirements should be gathered?
<--- Score

90. Has everyone on the team, including the team leaders, been properly trained?
<--- Score

91. How often are the team meetings?
<--- Score

92. What are the policy management tools use cases?
<--- Score

93. Does the scope remain the same?
<--- Score

94. How can the value of policy management tools be defined?
<--- Score

95. What are the policy management tools tasks and definitions?
<--- Score

96. What critical content must be communicated –

who, what, when, where, and how?
<--- Score

97. Is policy management tools linked to key stakeholder goals and objectives?
<--- Score

98. Has a high-level 'as is' process map been completed, verified and validated?
<--- Score

99. Who defines (or who defined) the rules and roles?
<--- Score

100. How does the policy management tools manager ensure against scope creep?
<--- Score

101. What is the definition of success?
<--- Score

102. Is special policy management tools user knowledge required?
<--- Score

103. What customer feedback methods were used to solicit their input?
<--- Score

104. What gets examined?
<--- Score

105. What would be the goal or target for a policy management tools's improvement team?
<--- Score

106. In what way can you redefine the criteria of choice clients have in your category in your favor?
<--- Score

107. How will variation in the actual durations of each activity be dealt with to ensure that the expected policy management tools results are met?
<--- Score

108. What sources do you use to gather information for a policy management tools study?
<--- Score

109. How are consistent policy management tools definitions important?
<--- Score

110. What are the boundaries of the scope? What is in bounds and what is not? What is the start point? What is the stop point?
<--- Score

111. Have all basic functions of policy management tools been defined?
<--- Score

112. What policy management tools services do you require?
<--- Score

113. Are different versions of process maps needed to account for the different types of inputs?
<--- Score

114. Has your scope been defined?
<--- Score

115. Is the work to date meeting requirements?
<--- Score

116. Is the team equipped with available and reliable resources?
<--- Score

117. What specifically is the problem? Where does it occur? When does it occur? What is its extent?
<--- Score

118. What is out of scope?
<--- Score

119. What is the scope of the policy management tools work?
<--- Score

120. Is the scope of policy management tools defined?
<--- Score

121. What are the Roles and Responsibilities for each team member and its leadership? Where is this documented?
<--- Score

122. Has a team charter been developed and communicated?
<--- Score

123. Will a policy management tools production readiness review be required?
<--- Score

124. What is the scope?
<--- Score

125. How would you define policy management tools leadership?
<--- Score

126. Do you all define policy management tools in the same way?
<--- Score

127. Has the direction changed at all during the course of policy management tools? If so, when did it change and why?
<--- Score

128. What scope to assess?
<--- Score

129. Are approval levels defined for contracts and supplements to contracts?
<--- Score

130. Do the problem and goal statements meet the SMART criteria (specific, measurable, attainable, relevant, and time-bound)?
<--- Score

131. What was the context?
<--- Score

132. Is there a clear policy management tools case definition?
<--- Score

133. Has a policy management tools requirement not

been met?

<--- Score

134. What intelligence can you gather?

<--- Score

135. Is there a completed, verified, and validated high-level 'as is' (not 'should be' or 'could be') stakeholder process map?

<--- Score

136. Are task requirements clearly defined?

<--- Score

137. Who is gathering policy management tools information?

<--- Score

138. What is the worst case scenario?

<--- Score

139. Is there regularly 100% attendance at the team meetings? If not, have appointed substitutes attended to preserve cross-functionality and full representation?

<--- Score

Add up total points for this section:
_ _ _ _ _ = Total points for this section

Divided by: _ _ _ _ _ _ (number of statements answered) = _ _ _ _ _ _
Average score for this section

Transfer your score to the policy management tools Index at the beginning of the Self-Assessment.

CRITERION #3: MEASURE:

INTENT: Gather the correct data.
Measure the current performance and
evolution of the situation.

In my belief, the answer to this
question is clearly defined:

5 Strongly Agree

4 Agree

3 Neutral

2 Disagree

1 Strongly Disagree

1. How do you measure efficient delivery of policy management tools services?
<--- Score

2. How can you manage cost down?
<--- Score

3. How is the value delivered by policy management tools being measured?

<--- Score

4. How do you verify if policy management tools is built right?
<--- Score

5. What are your customers expectations and measures?
<--- Score

6. How do you quantify and qualify impacts?
<--- Score

7. What is the policy management tools business impact?
<--- Score

8. Who is involved in verifying compliance?
<--- Score

9. What relevant entities could be measured?
<--- Score

10. What is measured? Why?
<--- Score

11. How is performance measured?
<--- Score

12. How are measurements made?
<--- Score

13. How can you reduce costs?
<--- Score

14. How can you measure policy management

tools in a systematic way?
<--- Score

15. Are there measurements based on task performance?
<--- Score

16. How do you verify the authenticity of the data and information used?
<--- Score

17. Will policy management tools have an impact on current business continuity, disaster recovery processes and/or infrastructure?
<--- Score

18. How much does it cost?
<--- Score

19. What are the costs and benefits?
<--- Score

20. Who pays the cost?
<--- Score

21. What would be a real cause for concern?
<--- Score

22. What causes mismanagement?
<--- Score

23. How can a policy management tools test verify your ideas or assumptions?
<--- Score

24. Are missed policy management tools

opportunities costing your organization money?
<--- Score

25. What does your operating model cost?
<--- Score

26. Are policy management tools vulnerabilities categorized and prioritized?
<--- Score

27. What are the costs of delaying policy management tools action?
<--- Score

28. What would it cost to replace your technology?
<--- Score

29. What could cause you to change course?
<--- Score

30. What are the policy management tools investment costs?
<--- Score

31. What do you measure and why?
<--- Score

32. What happens if cost savings do not materialize?
<--- Score

33. What is the cause of any policy management tools gaps?
<--- Score

34. Is there an opportunity to verify requirements?
<--- Score

35. Which costs should be taken into account?
<--- Score

36. Is it possible to estimate the impact of unanticipated complexity such as wrong or failed assumptions, feedback, etcetera on proposed reforms?
<--- Score

37. Are you aware of what could cause a problem?
<--- Score

38. How will success or failure be measured?
<--- Score

39. Has a cost center been established?
<--- Score

40. What drives O&M cost?
<--- Score

41. Do you have any cost policy management tools limitation requirements?
<--- Score

42. How do you verify and validate the policy management tools data?
<--- Score

43. Is the cost worth the policy management tools effort ?
<--- Score

44. What are your operating costs?
<--- Score

45. Do you have an issue in getting priority?
<--- Score

46. Do you verify that corrective actions were taken?
<--- Score

47. How do your measurements capture actionable policy management tools information for use in exceeding your customers expectations and securing your customers engagement?
<--- Score

48. What are the uncertainties surrounding estimates of impact?
<--- Score

49. How frequently do you track policy management tools measures?
<--- Score

50. What is an unallowable cost?
<--- Score

51. What are the strategic priorities for this year?
<--- Score

52. What is the total cost related to deploying policy management tools, including any consulting or professional services?
<--- Score

53. What does losing customers cost your organization?
<--- Score

54. What are the costs?
<--- Score

55. Are indirect costs charged to the policy management tools program?
<--- Score

56. Are supply costs steady or fluctuating?
<--- Score

57. What causes investor action?
<--- Score

58. What details are required of the policy management tools cost structure?
<--- Score

59. What are you verifying?
<--- Score

60. Do you effectively measure and reward individual and team performance?
<--- Score

61. What tests verify requirements?
<--- Score

62. What disadvantage does this cause for the user?
<--- Score

63. What causes extra work or rework?
<--- Score

64. Where is it measured?
<--- Score

65. What is your policy management tools quality cost segregation study?
<--- Score

66. Are the measurements objective?
<--- Score

67. Was a business case (cost/benefit) developed?
<--- Score

68. What are hidden policy management tools quality costs?
<--- Score

69. What measurements are being captured?
<--- Score

70. When should you bother with diagrams?
<--- Score

71. At what cost?
<--- Score

72. What is the root cause(s) of the problem?
<--- Score

73. How do you verify the policy management tools requirements quality?
<--- Score

74. Do the benefits outweigh the costs?
<--- Score

75. How do you aggregate measures across priorities?
<--- Score

76. How sensitive must the policy management tools strategy be to cost?
<--- Score

77. What is the total fixed cost?
<--- Score

78. Are actual costs in line with budgeted costs?
<--- Score

79. How do you measure success?
<--- Score

80. How can you reduce the costs of obtaining inputs?
<--- Score

81. What are allowable costs?
<--- Score

82. Are the policy management tools benefits worth its costs?
<--- Score

83. What are your primary costs, revenues, assets?
<--- Score

84. Are there any easy-to-implement alternatives to policy management tools? Sometimes other solutions are available that do not require the cost implications of a full-blown project?
<--- Score

85. Where can you go to verify the info?
<--- Score

86. What could cause delays in the schedule?

<--- Score

87. What is your decision requirements diagram?
<--- Score

88. Is the solution cost-effective?
<--- Score

89. What do people want to verify?
<--- Score

90. What does a Test Case verify?
<--- Score

91. Who should receive measurement reports?
<--- Score

92. Do you aggressively reward and promote the people who have the biggest impact on creating excellent policy management tools services/products?
<--- Score

93. When a disaster occurs, who gets priority?
<--- Score

94. Have you made assumptions about the shape of the future, particularly its impact on your customers and competitors?
<--- Score

95. What is the cost of rework?
<--- Score

96. Does a policy management tools quantification method exist?

<--- Score

97. Where is the cost?
<--- Score

98. How will you measure success?
<--- Score

99. What potential environmental factors impact the policy management tools effort?
<--- Score

100. How will measures be used to manage and adapt?
<--- Score

101. What can be used to verify compliance?
<--- Score

102. How do you measure lifecycle phases?
<--- Score

103. What are the operational costs after policy management tools deployment?
<--- Score

104. What evidence is there and what is measured?
<--- Score

105. What are the costs of reform?
<--- Score

106. Among the policy management tools product and service cost to be estimated, which is considered hardest to estimate?
<--- Score

107. Have design-to-cost goals been established?
<--- Score

108. How do you control the overall costs of your work processes?
<--- Score

109. Why do the measurements/indicators matter?
<--- Score

110. When are costs are incurred?
<--- Score

111. How do you verify your resources?
<--- Score

112. Are there competing policy management tools priorities?
<--- Score

113. Are the units of measure consistent?
<--- Score

114. What causes innovation to fail or succeed in your organization?
<--- Score

115. What methods are feasible and acceptable to estimate the impact of reforms?
<--- Score

116. How will you measure your policy management tools effectiveness?
<--- Score

117. What harm might be caused?
<--- Score

118. What are the estimated costs of proposed changes?
<--- Score

119. How will your organization measure success?
<--- Score

120. How long to keep data and how to manage retention costs?
<--- Score

121. Are you able to realize any cost savings?
<--- Score

122. How do you verify performance?
<--- Score

123. Why do you expend time and effort to implement measurement, for whom?
<--- Score

124. What are the current costs of the policy management tools process?
<--- Score

125. What does verifying compliance entail?
<--- Score

126. How do you measure variability?
<--- Score

127. How do you prevent mis-estimating cost?
<--- Score

128. What are the policy management tools key cost drivers?
<--- Score

129. Do you have a flow diagram of what happens?
<--- Score

130. Did you tackle the cause or the symptom?
<--- Score

131. How to cause the change?
<--- Score

Add up total points for this section:
_____ = Total points for this section

Divided by: _____ (number of statements answered) = _____
Average score for this section

Transfer your score to the policy management tools Index at the beginning of the Self-Assessment.

CRITERION #4: ANALYZE:

INTENT: Analyze causes, assumptions and hypotheses.

In my belief, the answer to this question is clearly defined:

5 Strongly Agree

4 Agree

3 Neutral

2 Disagree

1 Strongly Disagree

1. What information qualified as important?
<--- Score

2. How do you promote understanding that opportunity for improvement is not criticism of the status quo, or the people who created the status quo?
<--- Score

3. Do quality systems drive continuous improvement?
<--- Score

4. What resources go in to get the desired output?
<--- Score

5. Is there an established change management process?
<--- Score

6. What are the necessary qualifications?
<--- Score

7. Do your employees have the opportunity to do what they do best everyday?
<--- Score

8. Are you missing policy management tools opportunities?
<--- Score

9. How do you implement and manage your work processes to ensure that they meet design requirements?
<--- Score

10. What will drive policy management tools change?
<--- Score

11. Should you invest in industry-recognized qualifications?
<--- Score

12. What tools were used to generate the list of possible causes?
<--- Score

13. What policy management tools data should be

managed?
<--- Score

14. Is the gap/opportunity displayed and communicated in financial terms?
<--- Score

15. What process improvements will be needed?
<--- Score

16. How was the detailed process map generated, verified, and validated?
<--- Score

17. What were the financial benefits resulting from any 'ground fruit or low-hanging fruit' (quick fixes)?
<--- Score

18. Was a cause-and-effect diagram used to explore the different types of causes (or sources of variation)?
<--- Score

19. Do your contracts/agreements contain data security obligations?
<--- Score

20. How can risk management be tied procedurally to process elements?
<--- Score

21. How do you identify specific policy management tools investment opportunities and emerging trends?
<--- Score

22. Have you defined which data is gathered how?
<--- Score

23. How do you define collaboration and team output?
<--- Score

24. Who will facilitate the team and process?
<--- Score

25. What output to create?
<--- Score

26. Has data output been validated?
<--- Score

27. What are your best practices for minimizing policy management tools project risk, while demonstrating incremental value and quick wins throughout the policy management tools project lifecycle?
<--- Score

28. What are the personnel training and qualifications required?
<--- Score

29. What types of data do your policy management tools indicators require?
<--- Score

30. Think about the functions involved in your policy management tools project, what processes flow from these functions?
<--- Score

31. Were Pareto charts (or similar) used to portray the 'heavy hitters' (or key sources of variation)?
<--- Score

32. What is the output?
<--- Score

33. What does the data say about the performance of the stakeholder process?
<--- Score

34. How do you measure the operational performance of your key work systems and processes, including productivity, cycle time, and other appropriate measures of process effectiveness, efficiency, and innovation?
<--- Score

35. Do you have the authority to produce the output?
<--- Score

36. Were there any improvement opportunities identified from the process analysis?
<--- Score

37. A compounding model resolution with available relevant data can often provide insight towards a solution methodology; which policy management tools models, tools and techniques are necessary?
<--- Score

38. What is your organizations system for selecting qualified vendors?
<--- Score

39. What are your current levels and trends in key measures or indicators of policy management tools product and process performance that are important

to and directly serve your customers? How do these results compare with the performance of your competitors and other organizations with similar offerings?
<--- Score

40. How will the policy management tools data be captured?
<--- Score

41. Do several people in different organizational units assist with the policy management tools process?
<--- Score

42. What tools were used to narrow the list of possible causes?
<--- Score

43. What quality tools were used to get through the analyze phase?
<--- Score

44. Is there a strict change management process?
<--- Score

45. What policy management tools data do you gather or use now?
<--- Score

46. Is the required policy management tools data gathered?
<--- Score

47. What internal processes need improvement?
<--- Score

48. How do your work systems and key work processes relate to and capitalize on your core competencies?
<--- Score

49. What other jobs or tasks affect the performance of the steps in the policy management tools process?
<--- Score

50. How will the data be checked for quality?
<--- Score

51. Is the performance gap determined?
<--- Score

52. How many input/output points does it require?
<--- Score

53. What do you need to qualify?
<--- Score

54. How will the change process be managed?
<--- Score

55. Do you understand your management processes today?
<--- Score

56. Are policy management tools changes recognized early enough to be approved through the regular process?
<--- Score

57. What is your organizations process which leads to recognition of value generation?

<--- Score

58. Was a detailed process map created to amplify critical steps of the 'as is' stakeholder process?
<--- Score

59. How difficult is it to qualify what policy management tools ROI is?
<--- Score

60. How is the policy management tools Value Stream Mapping managed?
<--- Score

61. What policy management tools metrics are outputs of the process?
<--- Score

62. What data is gathered?
<--- Score

63. Is pre-qualification of suppliers carried out?
<--- Score

64. What qualifications are needed?
<--- Score

65. Record-keeping requirements flow from the records needed as inputs, outputs, controls and for transformation of a policy management tools process, are the records needed as inputs to the policy management tools process available?
<--- Score

66. What are the policy management tools business drivers?

<--- Score

67. What is the Value Stream Mapping?
<--- Score

68. How is the data gathered?
<--- Score

69. When should a process be art not science?
<--- Score

70. Is the final output clearly identified?
<--- Score

71. Who will gather what data?
<--- Score

72. Which policy management tools data should be retained?
<--- Score

73. What qualifies as competition?
<--- Score

74. What are the revised rough estimates of the financial savings/opportunity for policy management tools improvements?
<--- Score

75. Where is policy management tools data gathered?
<--- Score

76. Think about some of the processes you undertake within your organization, which do you own?
<--- Score

77. What is the cost of poor quality as supported by the team's analysis?
<--- Score

78. Has an output goal been set?
<--- Score

79. How much data can be collected in the given timeframe?
<--- Score

80. Is the suppliers process defined and controlled?
<--- Score

81. Have the problem and goal statements been updated to reflect the additional knowledge gained from the analyze phase?
<--- Score

82. How is policy management tools data gathered?
<--- Score

83. How often will data be collected for measures?
<--- Score

84. Were any designed experiments used to generate additional insight into the data analysis?
<--- Score

85. What are your outputs?
<--- Score

86. What are the best opportunities for value improvement?

<--- Score

87. What conclusions were drawn from the team's data collection and analysis? How did the team reach these conclusions?
<--- Score

88. Do your leaders quickly bounce back from setbacks?
<--- Score

89. What qualifications do policy management tools leaders need?
<--- Score

90. What were the crucial 'moments of truth' on the process map?
<--- Score

91. What methods do you use to gather policy management tools data?
<--- Score

92. What are your current levels and trends in key policy management tools measures or indicators of product and process performance that are important to and directly serve your customers?
<--- Score

93. What did the team gain from developing a sub-process map?
<--- Score

94. What successful thing are you doing today that may be blinding you to new growth opportunities?
<--- Score

95. Are your outputs consistent?
<--- Score

96. What controls do you have in place to protect data?
<--- Score

97. Do staff qualifications match your project?
<--- Score

98. How do you ensure that the policy management tools opportunity is realistic?
<--- Score

99. Is the policy management tools process severely broken such that a re-design is necessary?
<--- Score

100. What systems/processes must you excel at?
<--- Score

101. Who owns what data?
<--- Score

102. What training and qualifications will you need?
<--- Score

103. What, related to, policy management tools processes does your organization outsource?
<--- Score

104. What policy management tools data should be collected?
<--- Score

105. What are your key performance measures or indicators and in-process measures for the control and improvement of your policy management tools processes?
<--- Score

106. Is data and process analysis, root cause analysis and quantifying the gap/opportunity in place?
<--- Score

107. An organizationally feasible system request is one that considers the mission, goals and objectives of the organization, key questions are: is the policy management tools solution request practical and will it solve a problem or take advantage of an opportunity to achieve company goals?
<--- Score

108. How has the policy management tools data been gathered?
<--- Score

109. How does the organization define, manage, and improve its policy management tools processes?
<--- Score

110. How are outputs preserved and protected?
<--- Score

111. Can you add value to the current policy management tools decision-making process (largely qualitative) by incorporating uncertainty modeling (more quantitative)?
<--- Score

112. Where can you get qualified talent today?
<--- Score

113. What is the oversight process?
<--- Score

114. What is the complexity of the output produced?
<--- Score

115. Who is involved with workflow mapping?
<--- Score

116. Where is the data coming from to measure compliance?
<--- Score

117. What process should you select for improvement?
<--- Score

118. What other organizational variables, such as reward systems or communication systems, affect the performance of this policy management tools process?
<--- Score

119. Who is involved in the management review process?
<--- Score

120. What is the policy management tools Driver?
<--- Score

121. Are all team members qualified for all tasks?
<--- Score

122. What are your policy management tools processes?
<--- Score

123. What are the processes for audit reporting and management?
<--- Score

124. Who gets your output?
<--- Score

125. Do you, as a leader, bounce back quickly from setbacks?
<--- Score

126. What are the disruptive policy management tools technologies that enable your organization to radically change your business processes?
<--- Score

127. What kind of crime could a potential new hire have committed that would not only not disqualify him/her from being hired by your organization, but would actually indicate that he/she might be a particularly good fit?
<--- Score

128. Are all staff in core policy management tools subjects Highly Qualified?
<--- Score

129. What qualifications and skills do you need?
<--- Score

130. How is data used for program management and improvement?

<--- Score

131. How do mission and objectives affect the policy management tools processes of your organization?
<--- Score

132. Who qualifies to gain access to data?
<--- Score

Add up total points for this section:
_____ = Total points for this section

Divided by: _____ (number of statements answered) = _____
Average score for this section

Transfer your score to the policy management tools Index at the beginning of the Self-Assessment.

CRITERION #5: IMPROVE:

INTENT: Develop a practical solution. Innovate, establish and test the solution and to measure the results.

In my belief, the answer to this question is clearly defined:

5 Strongly Agree

4 Agree

3 Neutral

2 Disagree

1 Strongly Disagree

1. Are the risks fully understood, reasonable and manageable?
<--- Score

2. What went well, what should change, what can improve?
<--- Score

3. How do you manage policy management tools risk?

<--- Score

4. Do you need to do a usability evaluation?
<--- Score

5. Is the policy management tools solution sustainable?
<--- Score

6. Is the policy management tools documentation thorough?
<--- Score

7. How will you measure the results?
<--- Score

8. If you could go back in time five years, what decision would you make differently? What is your best guess as to what decision you're making today you might regret five years from now?
<--- Score

9. Is risk periodically assessed?
<--- Score

10. Can you identify any significant risks or exposures to policy management tools third- parties (vendors, service providers, alliance partners etc) that concern you?
<--- Score

11. Who manages supplier risk management in your organization?
<--- Score

12. What tools were used to tap into the creativity and

encourage 'outside the box' thinking?
<--- Score

13. What tools were used to evaluate the potential solutions?
<--- Score

14. Do you have the optimal project management team structure?
<--- Score

15. What improvements have been achieved?
<--- Score

16. How do you measure improved policy management tools service perception, and satisfaction?
<--- Score

17. How do you improve your likelihood of success ?
<--- Score

18. How does your organization evaluate strategic policy management tools success?
<--- Score

19. What are your current levels and trends in key measures or indicators of workforce and leader development?
<--- Score

20. Explorations of the frontiers of policy management tools will help you build influence, improve policy management tools, optimize decision making, and sustain change, what is your

approach?
<--- Score

21. Are the key business and technology risks being managed?
<--- Score

22. How do you decide how much to remunerate an employee?
<--- Score

23. What risks do you need to manage?
<--- Score

24. What policy management tools improvements can be made?
<--- Score

25. Have you achieved policy management tools improvements?
<--- Score

26. What criteria will you use to assess your policy management tools risks?
<--- Score

27. What is the team's contingency plan for potential problems occurring in implementation?
<--- Score

28. How do you link measurement and risk?
<--- Score

29. Are you assessing policy management tools and risk?
<--- Score

30. To what extent does management recognize policy management tools as a tool to increase the results?
<--- Score

31. What assumptions are made about the solution and approach?
<--- Score

32. What communications are necessary to support the implementation of the solution?
<--- Score

33. Do you cover the five essential competencies: Communication, Collaboration,Innovation, Adaptability, and Leadership that improve an organizations ability to leverage the new policy management tools in a volatile global economy?
<--- Score

34. Risk Identification: What are the possible risk events your organization faces in relation to policy management tools?
<--- Score

35. Is the solution technically practical?
<--- Score

36. What actually has to improve and by how much?
<--- Score

37. What lessons, if any, from a pilot were incorporated into the design of the full-scale solution?
<--- Score

38. What tools were most useful during the improve phase?
<--- Score

39. What does the 'should be' process map/design look like?
<--- Score

40. How do you define the solutions' scope?
<--- Score

41. How do you improve policy management tools service perception, and satisfaction?
<--- Score

42. Where do the policy management tools decisions reside?
<--- Score

43. How is knowledge sharing about risk management improved?
<--- Score

44. Do vendor agreements bring new compliance risk ?
<--- Score

45. Is the optimal solution selected based on testing and analysis?
<--- Score

46. What to do with the results or outcomes of measurements?
<--- Score

47. For decision problems, how do you develop a

decision statement?

<--- Score

48. What attendant changes will need to be made to ensure that the solution is successful?

<--- Score

49. How will you recognize and celebrate results?

<--- Score

50. Is there a cost/benefit analysis of optimal solution(s)?

<--- Score

51. What area needs the greatest improvement?

<--- Score

52. What needs improvement? Why?

<--- Score

53. Can the solution be designed and implemented within an acceptable time period?

<--- Score

54. Are procedures documented for managing policy management tools risks?

<--- Score

55. Who will be responsible for documenting the policy management tools requirements in detail?

<--- Score

56. Who controls the risk?

<--- Score

57. Are decisions made in a timely manner?

<--- Score

58. At what point will vulnerability assessments be performed once policy management tools is put into production (e.g., ongoing Risk Management after implementation)?
<--- Score

59. How do you deal with policy management tools risk?
<--- Score

60. When you map the key players in your own work and the types/domains of relationships with them, which relationships do you find easy and which challenging, and why?
<--- Score

61. Does the goal represent a desired result that can be measured?
<--- Score

62. Do those selected for the policy management tools team have a good general understanding of what policy management tools is all about?
<--- Score

63. How will you know that a change is an improvement?
<--- Score

64. What error proofing will be done to address some of the discrepancies observed in the 'as is' process?
<--- Score

65. What were the underlying assumptions on the

cost-benefit analysis?
<--- Score

66. Were any criteria developed to assist the team in testing and evaluating potential solutions?
<--- Score

67. Is the scope clearly documented?
<--- Score

68. Was a policy management tools charter developed?
<--- Score

69. policy management tools risk decisions: whose call Is It?
<--- Score

70. Is the policy management tools risk managed?
<--- Score

71. Who should make the policy management tools decisions?
<--- Score

72. What is the implementation plan?
<--- Score

73. Who will be responsible for making the decisions to include or exclude requested changes once policy management tools is underway?
<--- Score

74. Where do you need policy management tools improvement?
<--- Score

75. In the past few months, what is the smallest change you have made that has had the biggest positive result? What was it about that small change that produced the large return?
<--- Score

76. Who are the policy management tools decision-makers?
<--- Score

77. What strategies for policy management tools improvement are successful?
<--- Score

78. What is policy management tools risk?
<--- Score

79. Is there a small-scale pilot for proposed improvement(s)? What conclusions were drawn from the outcomes of a pilot?
<--- Score

80. What is the magnitude of the improvements?
<--- Score

81. How will you know that you have improved?
<--- Score

82. What are the concrete policy management tools results?
<--- Score

83. Is there a high likelihood that any recommendations will achieve their intended results?
<--- Score

84. How risky is your organization?
<--- Score

85. Is policy management tools documentation maintained?
<--- Score

86. Are the most efficient solutions problem-specific?
<--- Score

87. Which of the recognised risks out of all risks can be most likely transferred?
<--- Score

88. What can you do to improve?
<--- Score

89. What are the expected policy management tools results?
<--- Score

90. Is any policy management tools documentation required?
<--- Score

91. What current systems have to be understood and/or changed?
<--- Score

92. Who will be using the results of the measurement activities?
<--- Score

93. Does a good decision guarantee a good outcome?
<--- Score

94. Who do you report policy management tools results to?

<--- Score

95. How is continuous improvement applied to risk management?

<--- Score

96. What resources are required for the improvement efforts?

<--- Score

97. For estimation problems, how do you develop an estimation statement?

<--- Score

98. How do you mitigate policy management tools risk?

<--- Score

99. Can you integrate quality management and risk management?

<--- Score

100. What are the implications of the one critical policy management tools decision 10 minutes, 10 months, and 10 years from now?

<--- Score

101. What is the policy management tools's sustainability risk?

<--- Score

102. Who controls key decisions that will be made?

<--- Score

103. Risk events: what are the things that could go wrong?

<--- Score

104. How can skill-level changes improve policy management tools?

<--- Score

105. What is the risk?

<--- Score

106. Who are the key stakeholders for the policy management tools evaluation?

<--- Score

107. How are policy decisions made and where?

<--- Score

108. How will you know when its improved?

<--- Score

109. Is the measure of success for policy management tools understandable to a variety of people?

<--- Score

110. How do you keep improving policy management tools?

<--- Score

111. Who do you report policy management tools results to?

<--- Score

112. How can you improve performance?

<--- Score

113. What practices helps your organization to develop its capacity to recognize patterns?
<--- Score

114. How does the team improve its work?
<--- Score

115. Risk factors: what are the characteristics of policy management tools that make it risky?
<--- Score

116. What tools do you use once you have decided on a policy management tools strategy and more importantly how do you choose?
<--- Score

117. Which policy management tools solution is appropriate?
<--- Score

118. How do the policy management tools results compare with the performance of your competitors and other organizations with similar offerings?
<--- Score

119. Who makes the policy management tools decisions in your organization?
<--- Score

120. How do you go about comparing policy management tools approaches/solutions?
<--- Score

121. How do you improve productivity?
<--- Score

122. What are the affordable policy management tools risks?
<--- Score

123. How scalable is your policy management tools solution?
<--- Score

124. What is policy management tools's impact on utilizing the best solution(s)?
<--- Score

125. Is supporting policy management tools documentation required?
<--- Score

126. Would you develop a policy management tools Communication Strategy?
<--- Score

127. How can you better manage risk?
<--- Score

128. How can the phases of policy management tools development be identified?
<--- Score

129. What do you want to improve?
<--- Score

130. Was a pilot designed for the proposed solution(s)?
<--- Score

131. How are policy management tools risks managed?
<--- Score

132. How can you improve policy management tools?
<--- Score

133. How do you manage and improve your policy management tools work systems to deliver customer value and achieve organizational success and sustainability?
<--- Score

134. Are risk triggers captured?
<--- Score

135. Do you combine technical expertise with business knowledge and policy management tools Key topics include lifecycles, development approaches, requirements and how to make a business case?
<--- Score

136. Why improve in the first place?
<--- Score

137. Will the controls trigger any other risks?
<--- Score

138. How significant is the improvement in the eyes of the end user?
<--- Score

139. Have you identified breakpoints and/or risk tolerances that will trigger broad consideration of

a potential need for intervention or modification of strategy?
<--- Score

140. Who are the people involved in developing and implementing policy management tools?
<--- Score

141. What should a proof of concept or pilot accomplish?
<--- Score

142. How do you measure progress and evaluate training effectiveness?
<--- Score

Add up total points for this section:
_ _ _ _ _ = Total points for this section

Divided by: _ _ _ _ _ _ (number of statements answered) = _ _ _ _ _ _
Average score for this section

Transfer your score to the policy management tools Index at the beginning of the Self-Assessment.

CRITERION #6: CONTROL:

INTENT: Implement the practical solution. Maintain the performance and correct possible complications.

In my belief, the answer to this question is clearly defined:

5 Strongly Agree

4 Agree

3 Neutral

2 Disagree

1 Strongly Disagree

1. How is policy management tools project cost planned, managed, monitored?
<--- Score

2. Is new knowledge gained imbedded in the response plan?
<--- Score

3. What should the next improvement project be that

is related to policy management tools?
<--- Score

4. What is the recommended frequency of auditing?
<--- Score

5. How do you establish and deploy modified action plans if circumstances require a shift in plans and rapid execution of new plans?
<--- Score

6. Are suggested corrective/restorative actions indicated on the response plan for known causes to problems that might surface?
<--- Score

7. What are customers monitoring?
<--- Score

8. Does policy management tools appropriately measure and monitor risk?
<--- Score

9. What policy management tools standards are applicable?
<--- Score

10. Where do ideas that reach policy makers and planners as proposals for policy management tools strengthening and reform actually originate?
<--- Score

11. How likely is the current policy management tools plan to come in on schedule or on budget?
<--- Score

12. In the case of a policy management tools project, the criteria for the audit derive from implementation objectives, an audit of a policy management tools project involves assessing whether the recommendations outlined for implementation have been met, can you track that any policy management tools project is implemented as planned, and is it working?
<--- Score

13. Has the improved process and its steps been standardized?
<--- Score

14. Is there documentation that will support the successful operation of the improvement?
<--- Score

15. What are your results for key measures or indicators of the accomplishment of your policy management tools strategy and action plans, including building and strengthening core competencies?
<--- Score

16. Is knowledge gained on process shared and institutionalized?
<--- Score

17. Does the response plan contain a definite closed loop continual improvement scheme (e.g., plan-do-check-act)?
<--- Score

18. How do controls support value?
<--- Score

19. Will any special training be provided for results interpretation?
<--- Score

20. What is your plan to assess your security risks?
<--- Score

21. Can you adapt and adjust to changing policy management tools situations?
<--- Score

22. What are the critical parameters to watch?
<--- Score

23. What is the standard for acceptable policy management tools performance?
<--- Score

24. How will new or emerging customer needs/requirements be checked/communicated to orient the process toward meeting the new specifications and continually reducing variation?
<--- Score

25. Does a troubleshooting guide exist or is it needed?
<--- Score

26. How is change control managed?
<--- Score

27. Is there a control plan in place for sustaining improvements (short and long-term)?
<--- Score

28. How do you spread information?

<--- Score

29. Does the policy management tools performance meet the customer's requirements?
<--- Score

30. Is there a transfer of ownership and knowledge to process owner and process team tasked with the responsibilities.
<--- Score

31. How do your controls stack up?
<--- Score

32. How will policy management tools decisions be made and monitored?
<--- Score

33. What is the best design framework for policy management tools organization now that, in a post industrial-age if the top-down, command and control model is no longer relevant?
<--- Score

34. What is the control/monitoring plan?
<--- Score

35. How will you measure your QA plan's effectiveness?
<--- Score

36. Are the planned controls in place?
<--- Score

37. Is reporting being used or needed?
<--- Score

38. How widespread is its use?
<--- Score

39. Is there a recommended audit plan for routine surveillance inspections of policy management tools's gains?
<--- Score

40. How will report readings be checked to effectively monitor performance?
<--- Score

41. Have new or revised work instructions resulted?
<--- Score

42. What do your reports reflect?
<--- Score

43. Implementation Planning: is a pilot needed to test the changes before a full roll out occurs?
<--- Score

44. Are pertinent alerts monitored, analyzed and distributed to appropriate personnel?
<--- Score

45. Are documented procedures clear and easy to follow for the operators?
<--- Score

46. How will the process owner verify improvement in present and future sigma levels, process capabilities?
<--- Score

47. How can you best use all of your knowledge

repositories to enhance learning and sharing?
<--- Score

48. Who has control over resources?
<--- Score

49. Who controls critical resources?
<--- Score

50. Are you measuring, monitoring and predicting policy management tools activities to optimize operations and profitability, and enhancing outcomes?
<--- Score

51. How do you plan for the cost of succession?
<--- Score

52. Are controls in place and consistently applied?
<--- Score

53. How do senior leaders actions reflect a commitment to the organizations policy management tools values?
<--- Score

54. Is there a documented and implemented monitoring plan?
<--- Score

55. Are the policy management tools standards challenging?
<--- Score

56. What are you attempting to measure/monitor?
<--- Score

57. What is your theory of human motivation, and how does your compensation plan fit with that view?
<--- Score

58. Is there a standardized process?
<--- Score

59. Against what alternative is success being measured?
<--- Score

60. What do you measure to verify effectiveness gains?
<--- Score

61. What are the key elements of your policy management tools performance improvement system, including your evaluation, organizational learning, and innovation processes?
<--- Score

62. Who is the policy management tools process owner?
<--- Score

63. Is the policy management tools test/monitoring cost justified?
<--- Score

64. Does job training on the documented procedures need to be part of the process team's education and training?
<--- Score

65. How will the day-to-day responsibilities for

monitoring and continual improvement be transferred from the improvement team to the process owner?
<--- Score

66. What are the known security controls?
<--- Score

67. Are operating procedures consistent?
<--- Score

68. Is there a policy management tools Communication plan covering who needs to get what information when?
<--- Score

69. Who is going to spread your message?
<--- Score

70. Will your goals reflect your program budget?
<--- Score

71. What other systems, operations, processes, and infrastructures (hiring practices, staffing, training, incentives/rewards, metrics/dashboards/scorecards, etc.) need updates, additions, changes, or deletions in order to facilitate knowledge transfer and improvements?
<--- Score

72. You may have created your quality measures at a time when you lacked resources, technology wasn't up to the required standard, or low service levels were the industry norm. Have those circumstances changed?
<--- Score

73. How will input, process, and output variables be checked to detect for sub-optimal conditions?
<--- Score

74. Will the team be available to assist members in planning investigations?
<--- Score

75. Do you monitor the policy management tools decisions made and fine tune them as they evolve?
<--- Score

76. Has the policy management tools value of standards been quantified?
<--- Score

77. Can support from partners be adjusted?
<--- Score

78. How do you encourage people to take control and responsibility?
<--- Score

79. What can you control?
<--- Score

80. How will the process owner and team be able to hold the gains?
<--- Score

81. What quality tools were useful in the control phase?
<--- Score

82. Are the planned controls working?

<--- Score

83. What should you measure to verify efficiency gains?
<--- Score

84. Act/Adjust: What Do you Need to Do Differently?
<--- Score

85. Is a response plan established and deployed?
<--- Score

86. Do the policy management tools decisions you make today help people and the planet tomorrow?
<--- Score

87. Do you monitor the effectiveness of your policy management tools activities?
<--- Score

88. Are new process steps, standards, and documentation ingrained into normal operations?
<--- Score

89. What other areas of the group might benefit from the policy management tools team's improvements, knowledge, and learning?
<--- Score

90. Are there documented procedures?
<--- Score

91. Is there an action plan in case of emergencies?
<--- Score

92. Who sets the policy management tools

standards?
<--- Score

93. How do you plan on providing proper recognition and disclosure of supporting companies?
<--- Score

94. Will existing staff require re-training, for example, to learn new business processes?
<--- Score

95. How might the group capture best practices and lessons learned so as to leverage improvements?
<--- Score

96. Is a response plan in place for when the input, process, or output measures indicate an 'out-of-control' condition?
<--- Score

97. What key inputs and outputs are being measured on an ongoing basis?
<--- Score

Add up total points for this section:
_ _ _ _ _ = Total points for this section

Divided by: _ _ _ _ _ _ (number of statements answered) = _ _ _ _ _ _
Average score for this section

Transfer your score to the policy management tools Index at the beginning of the Self-Assessment.

CRITERION #7: SUSTAIN:

INTENT: Retain the benefits.

In my belief, the answer to this question is clearly defined:

5 Strongly Agree

4 Agree

3 Neutral

2 Disagree

1 Strongly Disagree

1. Is maximizing policy management tools protection the same as minimizing policy management tools loss?
<--- Score

2. In a project to restructure policy management tools outcomes, which stakeholders would you involve?
<--- Score

3. What are strategies for increasing support and reducing opposition?

<--- Score

4. How do senior leaders deploy your organizations vision and values through your leadership system, to the workforce, to key suppliers and partners, and to customers and other stakeholders, as appropriate?
<--- Score

5. What goals did you miss?
<--- Score

6. If your company went out of business tomorrow, would anyone who doesn't get a paycheck here care?
<--- Score

7. What is the source of the strategies for policy management tools strengthening and reform?
<--- Score

8. Which functions and people interact with the supplier and or customer?
<--- Score

9. How can you negotiate policy management tools successfully with a stubborn boss, an irate client, or a deceitful coworker?
<--- Score

10. Whose voice (department, ethnic group, women, older workers, etc) might you have missed hearing from in your company, and how might you amplify this voice to create positive momentum for your business?
<--- Score

11. Have benefits been optimized with all key stakeholders?
<--- Score

12. If you got fired and a new hire took your place, what would she do different?
<--- Score

13. Why is it important to have senior management support for a policy management tools project?
<--- Score

14. Do you see more potential in people than they do in themselves?
<--- Score

15. What are specific policy management tools rules to follow?
<--- Score

16. Who is responsible for policy management tools?
<--- Score

17. If you find that you havent accomplished one of the goals for one of the steps of the policy management tools strategy, what will you do to fix it?
<--- Score

18. What should you stop doing?
<--- Score

19. What was the last experiment you ran?
<--- Score

20. How do you assess the policy management tools pitfalls that are inherent in implementing it?
<--- Score

21. What is the kind of project structure that would be appropriate for your policy management tools project, should it be formal and complex, or can it be less formal and relatively simple?
<--- Score

22. Are you changing as fast as the world around you?
<--- Score

23. How do you provide a safe environment -physically and emotionally?
<--- Score

24. How are you doing compared to your industry?
<--- Score

25. What is the estimated value of the project?
<--- Score

26. How will you motivate the stakeholders with the least vested interest?
<--- Score

27. How will you know that the policy management tools project has been successful?
<--- Score

28. How do you engage the workforce, in addition to satisfying them?
<--- Score

29. Is policy management tools dependent on the

successful delivery of a current project?
<--- Score

30. Are the criteria for selecting recommendations stated?
<--- Score

31. How do you manage policy management tools Knowledge Management (KM)?
<--- Score

32. Who will be responsible for deciding whether policy management tools goes ahead or not after the initial investigations?
<--- Score

33. What relationships among policy management tools trends do you perceive?
<--- Score

34. What are the usability implications of policy management tools actions?
<--- Score

35. How do you accomplish your long range policy management tools goals?
<--- Score

36. Do you say no to customers for no reason?
<--- Score

37. What is it like to work for you?
<--- Score

38. Are there any activities that you can take off your to do list?

<--- Score

39. Who are your customers?
<--- Score

40. How do you track customer value, profitability or financial return, organizational success, and sustainability?
<--- Score

41. Marketing budgets are tighter, consumers are more skeptical, and social media has changed forever the way we talk about policy management tools, how do you gain traction?
<--- Score

42. What is your policy management tools strategy?
<--- Score

43. Are the assumptions believable and achievable?
<--- Score

44. What do we do when new problems arise?
<--- Score

45. How much contingency will be available in the budget?
<--- Score

46. Have new benefits been realized?
<--- Score

47. Is a policy management tools breakthrough on the horizon?
<--- Score

48. How important is policy management tools to the user organizations mission?
<--- Score

49. What you are going to do to affect the numbers?
<--- Score

50. Do you know who is a friend or a foe?
<--- Score

51. Are you relevant? Will you be relevant five years from now? Ten?
<--- Score

52. Are you using a design thinking approach and integrating Innovation, policy management tools Experience, and Brand Value?
<--- Score

53. How do you lead with policy management tools in mind?
<--- Score

54. What are the key enablers to make this policy management tools move?
<--- Score

55. Is your basic point _____ or _____?
<--- Score

56. What counts that you are not counting?
<--- Score

57. If there were zero limitations, what would you

do differently?
<--- Score

58. What stupid rule would you most like to kill?
<--- Score

59. How do you ensure that implementations of policy management tools products are done in a way that ensures safety?
<--- Score

60. What is a feasible sequencing of reform initiatives over time?
<--- Score

61. Operational - will it work?
<--- Score

62. Is the impact that policy management tools has shown?
<--- Score

63. Is policy management tools realistic, or are you setting yourself up for failure?
<--- Score

64. Why should people listen to you?
<--- Score

65. Is there any existing policy management tools governance structure?
<--- Score

66. Why will customers want to buy your organizations products/services?
<--- Score

67. What are the short and long-term policy management tools goals?

<--- Score

68. How do you govern and fulfill your societal responsibilities?

<--- Score

69. How do you proactively clarify deliverables and policy management tools quality expectations?

<--- Score

70. How can you become the company that would put you out of business?

<--- Score

71. What are the barriers to increased policy management tools production?

<--- Score

72. Do you feel that more should be done in the policy management tools area?

<--- Score

73. What is something you believe that nearly no one agrees with you on?

<--- Score

74. How do you foster innovation?

<--- Score

75. Do you know what you are doing? And who do you call if you don't?

<--- Score

76. What does your signature ensure?
<--- Score

77. Are you making progress, and are you making progress as policy management tools leaders?
<--- Score

78. What policy management tools modifications can you make work for you?
<--- Score

79. What is your BATNA (best alternative to a negotiated agreement)?
<--- Score

80. What is your question? Why?
<--- Score

81. How do you determine the key elements that affect policy management tools workforce satisfaction, how are these elements determined for different workforce groups and segments?
<--- Score

82. What is effective policy management tools?
<--- Score

83. Which individuals, teams or departments will be involved in policy management tools?
<--- Score

84. What are the top 3 things at the forefront of your policy management tools agendas for the next 3 years?
<--- Score

85. Can you break it down?
<--- Score

86. Is your strategy driving your strategy? Or is the way in which you allocate resources driving your strategy?
<--- Score

87. Would you rather sell to knowledgeable and informed customers or to uninformed customers?
<--- Score

88. Do you have past policy management tools successes?
<--- Score

89. How can you incorporate support to ensure safe and effective use of policy management tools into the services that you provide?
<--- Score

90. How do you cross-sell and up-sell your policy management tools success?
<--- Score

91. If your customer were your grandmother, would you tell her to buy what you're selling?
<--- Score

92. Who do you think the world wants your organization to be?
<--- Score

93. Do you think policy management tools accomplishes the goals you expect it to accomplish?
<--- Score

94. What would you recommend your friend do if he/she were facing this dilemma?
<--- Score

95. Instead of going to current contacts for new ideas, what if you reconnected with dormant contacts-- the people you used to know? If you were going reactivate a dormant tie, who would it be?
<--- Score

96. Do policy management tools rules make a reasonable demand on a users capabilities?
<--- Score

97. What are the success criteria that will indicate that policy management tools objectives have been met and the benefits delivered?
<--- Score

98. What could happen if you do not do it?
<--- Score

99. How do you go about securing policy management tools?
<--- Score

100. Is the policy management tools organization completing tasks effectively and efficiently?
<--- Score

101. To whom do you add value?
<--- Score

102. What is the overall business strategy?
<--- Score

103. How do you stay inspired?
<--- Score

104. What are the performance and scale of the policy management tools tools?
<--- Score

105. What unique value proposition (UVP) do you offer?
<--- Score

106. If no one would ever find out about your accomplishments, how would you lead differently?
<--- Score

107. Can you do all this work?
<--- Score

108. Is a policy management tools team work effort in place?
<--- Score

109. How will you insure seamless interoperability of policy management tools moving forward?
<--- Score

110. What is the craziest thing you can do?
<--- Score

111. Has implementation been effective in reaching specified objectives so far?
<--- Score

112. How do you make it meaningful in connecting policy management tools with what users do day-

to-day?
<--- Score

113. What happens at your organization when people fail?
<--- Score

114. Were lessons learned captured and communicated?
<--- Score

115. What are your most important goals for the strategic policy management tools objectives?
<--- Score

116. Who will provide the final approval of policy management tools deliverables?
<--- Score

117. What would have to be true for the option on the table to be the best possible choice?
<--- Score

118. Is it economical; do you have the time and money?
<--- Score

119. How do you create buy-in?
<--- Score

120. What information is critical to your organization that your executives are ignoring?
<--- Score

121. Do you think you know, or do you know you know ?

<--- Score

122. Who is on the team?
<--- Score

123. Whom among your colleagues do you trust, and for what?
<--- Score

124. At what moment would you think; Will I get fired?
<--- Score

125. How will you ensure you get what you expected?
<--- Score

126. If you had to leave your organization for a year and the only communication you could have with employees/colleagues was a single paragraph, what would you write?
<--- Score

127. Who uses your product in ways you never expected?
<--- Score

128. Do you have the right capabilities and capacities?
<--- Score

129. Are you paying enough attention to the partners your company depends on to succeed?
<--- Score

130. What happens if you do not have enough funding?
<--- Score

131. Are your responses positive or negative?
<--- Score

132. What are the business goals policy management tools is aiming to achieve?
<--- Score

133. What new services of functionality will be implemented next with policy management tools ?
<--- Score

134. Political -is anyone trying to undermine this project?
<--- Score

135. What are the essentials of internal policy management tools management?
<--- Score

136. Who are four people whose careers you have enhanced?
<--- Score

137. What have you done to protect your business from competitive encroachment?
<--- Score

138. Who have you, as a company, historically been when you've been at your best?
<--- Score

139. Who will manage the integration of tools?
<--- Score

140. If you were responsible for initiating and implementing major changes in your organization,

what steps might you take to ensure acceptance of those changes?
<--- Score

141. Are you satisfied with your current role? If not, what is missing from it?
<--- Score

142. How long will it take to change?
<--- Score

143. In retrospect, of the projects that you pulled the plug on, what percent do you wish had been allowed to keep going, and what percent do you wish had ended earlier?
<--- Score

144. Where can you break convention?
<--- Score

145. Which models, tools and techniques are necessary?
<--- Score

146. How do you deal with policy management tools changes?
<--- Score

147. What are you trying to prove to yourself, and how might it be hijacking your life and business success?
<--- Score

148. Ask yourself: how would you do this work if you only had one staff member to do it?
<--- Score

149. What is your competitive advantage?
<--- Score

150. Do you have the right people on the bus?
<--- Score

151. What knowledge, skills and characteristics mark a good policy management tools project manager?
<--- Score

152. When information truly is ubiquitous, when reach and connectivity are completely global, when computing resources are infinite, and when a whole new set of impossibilities are not only possible, but happening, what will that do to your business?
<--- Score

153. What are internal and external policy management tools relations?
<--- Score

154. Are new benefits received and understood?
<--- Score

155. How likely is it that a customer would recommend your company to a friend or colleague?
<--- Score

156. Who will determine interim and final deadlines?
<--- Score

157. What projects are going on in the organization today, and what resources are those projects using from the resource pools?
<--- Score

158. Who else should you help?
<--- Score

159. What is the purpose of policy management tools in relation to the mission?
<--- Score

160. What is the range of capabilities?
<--- Score

161. How can you become more high-tech but still be high touch?
<--- Score

162. What management system can you use to leverage the policy management tools experience, ideas, and concerns of the people closest to the work to be done?
<--- Score

163. Who do we want your customers to become?
<--- Score

164. Who is the main stakeholder, with ultimate responsibility for driving policy management tools forward?
<--- Score

165. What is an unauthorized commitment?
<--- Score

166. Why should you adopt a policy management tools framework?
<--- Score

167. What have been your experiences in defining long range policy management tools goals?
<--- Score

168. What business benefits will policy management tools goals deliver if achieved?
<--- Score

169. How do you set policy management tools stretch targets and how do you get people to not only participate in setting these stretch targets but also that they strive to achieve these?
<--- Score

170. What is the overall talent health of your organization as a whole at senior levels, and for each organization reporting to a member of the Senior Leadership Team?
<--- Score

171. If you do not follow, then how to lead?
<--- Score

172. How do you listen to customers to obtain actionable information?
<--- Score

173. How do you keep the momentum going?
<--- Score

174. Who do you want your customers to become?
<--- Score

175. Will it be accepted by users?
<--- Score

176. Can the schedule be done in the given time?
<--- Score

177. What will be the consequences to the stakeholder (financial, reputation etc) if policy management tools does not go ahead or fails to deliver the objectives?
<--- Score

178. What are the challenges?
<--- Score

179. What is the funding source for this project?
<--- Score

180. Why not do policy management tools?
<--- Score

181. What is the recommended frequency of auditing?
<--- Score

182. What are the gaps in your knowledge and experience?
<--- Score

183. How much does policy management tools help?
<--- Score

184. What one word do you want to own in the minds of your customers, employees, and partners?
<--- Score

185. Can you maintain your growth without detracting from the factors that have contributed to your success?
<--- Score

186. If you weren't already in this business, would you enter it today? And if not, what are you going to do about it?
<--- Score

187. Who, on the executive team or the board, has spoken to a customer recently?
<--- Score

188. How do you keep records, of what?
<--- Score

189. Who is responsible for errors?
<--- Score

190. Did your employees make progress today?
<--- Score

191. What may be the consequences for the performance of an organization if all stakeholders are not consulted regarding policy management tools?
<--- Score

192. Do you have an implicit bias for capital investments over people investments?
<--- Score

193. What role does communication play in the success or failure of a policy management tools project?
<--- Score

194. How do you transition from the baseline to the target?
<--- Score

195. Is there a work around that you can use?
<--- Score

196. What are you challenging?
<--- Score

197. Are assumptions made in policy management tools stated explicitly?
<--- Score

198. What is the big policy management tools idea?
<--- Score

199. What are the potential basics of policy management tools fraud?
<--- Score

200. What did you miss in the interview for the worst hire you ever made?
<--- Score

201. How does policy management tools integrate with other stakeholder initiatives?
<--- Score

202. How do customers see your organization?
<--- Score

203. What happens when a new employee joins the organization?
<--- Score

204. Are you / should you be revolutionary or evolutionary?
<--- Score

205. Think of your policy management tools project, what are the main functions?
<--- Score

206. What must you excel at?
<--- Score

207. How do you know if you are successful?
<--- Score

Add up total points for this section:
_ _ _ _ _ = Total points for this section

Divided by: _ _ _ _ _ _ (number of statements answered) = _ _ _ _ _ _
Average score for this section

Transfer your score to the policy management tools Index at the beginning of the Self-Assessment.

Policy Management Tools and Managing Projects, Criteria for Project Managers:

1.0 Initiating Process Group: Policy Management Tools

1. Who are the Policy Management Tools project stakeholders?

2. What communication items need improvement?

3. Mitigate. what will you do to minimize the impact should the risk event occur?

4. Information sharing?

5. What were the challenges that you encountered during the execution of a previous Policy Management Tools project that you would not want to repeat?

6. Do you know the roles & responsibilities required for this Policy Management Tools project?

7. Who is behind the Policy Management Tools project?

8. What must be done?

9. Did the Policy Management Tools project team have the right skills?

10. Are the Policy Management Tools project team and stakeholders meeting regularly and using a meeting agenda and taking notes to accurately document what is being covered and what happened in the weekly meetings?

11. The process to Manage Stakeholders is part of which process group?

12. Were escalated issues resolved promptly?

13. How do you help others satisfy needs?

14. Were decisions made in a timely manner?

15. Do you know all the stakeholders impacted by the Policy Management Tools project and what needs are?

16. What do you need to do?

17. During which stage of Risk planning are risks prioritized based on probability and impact?

18. How can you make your needs known?

19. Do you know the Policy Management Tools projects goal, purpose and objectives?

20. Are identified risks being monitored properly, are new risks arising during the Policy Management Tools project or are foreseen risks occurring?

1.1 Project Charter: Policy Management Tools

21. What barriers do you predict to your success?

22. How are Policy Management Tools projects different from operations?

23. What is the business need?

24. Why the improvements?

25. When do you use a Policy Management Tools project Charter?

26. Review the general mission What system will be affected by the improvement efforts?

27. What are the assumptions?

28. When will this occur?

29. What is the justification?

30. What are the deliverables?

31. Why is a Policy Management Tools project Charter used?

32. How will you learn more about the process or system you are trying to improve?

33. Are you building in-house ?

34. What are you trying to accomplish?

35. Why do you need to manage scope?

36. Policy Management Tools project objective statement: what must the Policy Management Tools project do?

37. Why have you chosen the aim you have set forth?

38. Why is it important?

39. Where does all this information come from?

40. What changes can you make to improve?

1.2 Stakeholder Register: Policy Management Tools

41. Is your organization ready for change?

42. What opportunities exist to provide communications?

43. Who are the stakeholders?

44. How will reports be created?

45. How much influence do they have on the Policy Management Tools project?

46. What are the major Policy Management Tools project milestones requiring communications or providing communications opportunities?

47. Who wants to talk about Security?

48. How should employers make voices heard?

49. How big is the gap?

50. What & Why?

51. What is the power of the stakeholder?

52. Who is managing stakeholder engagement?

1.3 Stakeholder Analysis Matrix: Policy Management Tools

53. Who influences whom?

54. Usps (unique selling points)?

55. Are the required specifications for products or services changing?

56. How do customers express needs?

57. Why is it important to identify them?

58. Political effects?

59. How will the Policy Management Tools project benefit them?

60. Sustaining internal capabilities?

61. Morale, commitment, leadership?

62. What should thwe organizations stakeholders avoid?

63. What is your Advocacy Strategy?

64. Is there a reason why you are or are not not using an external rating system?

65. How will the stakeholder directly benefit from the Policy Management Tools project and how will this

affect the stakeholders motivation?

66. Economy - home, abroad?

67. Vulnerable groups; who are the vulnerable groups that might be affected by the Policy Management Tools project?

68. Marketing - reach, distribution, awareness?

69. Who has been involved in the area (thematic or geographic) in the past?

70. Competitors vulnerabilities?

71. Inoculations or payment to receive them?

72. New markets, vertical, horizontal?

2.0 Planning Process Group: Policy Management Tools

73. Are there efficient coordination mechanisms to avoid overloading the counterparts, participating stakeholders?

74. How many days can task X be late in starting without affecting the Policy Management Tools project completion date?

75. How will users learn how to use the deliverables?

76. To what extent is the program helping to influence your organizations policy framework?

77. If task x starts two days late, what is the effect on the Policy Management Tools project end date?

78. Will you be replaced?

79. What is the NEXT thing to do?

80. Is the pace of implementing the products of the program ensuring the completeness of the results of the Policy Management Tools project?

81. You did your readings, yes?

82. What is the critical path for this Policy Management Tools project, and what is the duration of the critical path?

83. In what way has the program contributed towards the issue culture and development included on the public agenda?

84. The Policy Management Tools project charter is created in which Policy Management Tools project management process group?

85. Why do it Policy Management Tools projects fail?

86. How will you know you did it?

87. How are the principles of aid effectiveness (ownership, alignment, management for development results and mutual responsibility) being applied in the Policy Management Tools project?

88. If a risk event occurs, what will you do?

89. Do the partners have sufficient financial capacity to keep up the benefits produced by the programme?

90. When will the Policy Management Tools project be done?

91. To what extent have the target population and participants made the activities own, taking an active role in it?

92. Product breakdown structure (pbs): what is the Policy Management Tools project result or product, and how should it look like, what are its parts?

2.1 Project Management Plan: Policy Management Tools

93. How do you organize the costs in the Policy Management Tools project management plan?

94. What worked well?

95. If the Policy Management Tools project management plan is a comprehensive document that guides you in Policy Management Tools project execution and control, then what should it NOT contain?

96. Who manages integration?

97. What should you drop in order to add something new?

98. Does the implementation plan have an appropriate division of responsibilities?

99. Are alternatives safe, functional, constructible, economical, reasonable and sustainable?

100. How can you best help your organization to develop consistent practices in Policy Management Tools project management planning stages?

101. What does management expect of PMs?

102. What are the assigned resources?

103. Is the appropriate plan selected based on your organizations objectives and evaluation criteria expressed in Principles and Guidelines policies?

104. What is Policy Management Tools project scope management?

105. Why Change?

106. Is the budget realistic?

107. Are there any Client staffing expectations?

108. Who is the sponsor?

109. Why do you manage integration?

110. Do there need to be organizational changes?

111. When is a Policy Management Tools project management plan created?

2.2 Scope Management Plan: Policy Management Tools

112. Is mitigation authorized or recommended?

113. How do you handle uncertainty or conflict?

114. Timeline and milestones?

115. Is pert / critical path or equivalent methodology being used?

116. Has the business need been clearly defined?

117. Are funding resource estimates sufficiently detailed and documented for use in planning and tracking the Policy Management Tools project?

118. What are the risks that could significantly affect the resources needed for the Policy Management Tools project?

119. Was the scope definition used in task sequencing?

120. Sensitivity analysis?

121. Does the resource management plan include a personnel development plan?

122. What are the Quality Assurance overheads?

123. Are corrective actions taken when actual results

are substantially different from detailed Policy Management Tools project plan (variances)?

124. Is there an issues management plan in place?

125. Are cause and effect determined for risks when they occur?

126. What are the risks of not having good inter-organization cooperation on the Policy Management Tools project?

127. Is there an on-going process in place to monitor Policy Management Tools project risks?

128. Will your organizations estimating methodology be used and followed?

129. To whom will the deliverables be first presented for inspection and verification?

130. Are mitigation strategies identified?

131. Are target dates established for each milestone deliverable?

2.3 Requirements Management Plan: Policy Management Tools

132. How do you know that you have done this right?

133. Did you get proper approvals?

134. Do you have price sheets and a methodology for determining the total proposal cost?

135. Will the Policy Management Tools project requirements become approved in writing?

136. How knowledgeable is the team in the proposed application area?

137. What went right?

138. Do you understand the role that each stakeholder will play in the requirements process?

139. Could inaccurate or incomplete requirements in this Policy Management Tools project create a serious risk for the business?

140. Describe the process for rejecting the Policy Management Tools project requirements. Who has the authority to reject Policy Management Tools project requirements?

141. The wbs is developed as part of a joint planning session. and how do you know that youhave done this right?

142. Will you use tracing to help understand the impact of a change in requirements?

143. What cost metrics will be used?

144. Why manage requirements?

145. Controlling Policy Management Tools project requirements involves monitoring the status of the Policy Management Tools project requirements and managing changes to the requirements. Who is responsible for monitoring and tracking the Policy Management Tools project requirements?

146. Is it new or replacing an existing business system or process?

147. After the requirements are gathered and set forth on the requirements register, theyre little more than a laundry list of items. Some may be duplicates, some might conflict with others and some will be too broad or too vague to understand. Describe how the requirements will be analyzed. Who will perform the analysis?

148. In case of software development; Should you have a test for each code module?

149. Business analysis scope?

150. When and how will a requirements baseline be established in this Policy Management Tools project?

151. Are actual resource expenditures versus planned still acceptable?

2.4 Requirements Documentation: Policy Management Tools

152. Do your constraints stand?

153. Have the benefits identified with the system being identified clearly?

154. Are all functions required by the customer included?

155. How will they be documented / shared?

156. Are there legal issues?

157. Can the requirements be checked?

158. What is effective documentation?

159. How much does requirements engineering cost?

160. Where do you define what is a customer, what are the attributes of customer?

161. Is your business case still valid?

162. Has requirements gathering uncovered information that would necessitate changes?

163. What kind of entity is a problem ?

164. How can you document system requirements?

165. The problem with gathering requirements is right there in the word gathering. What images does it conjure?

166. What can tools do for us?

167. How will requirements be documented and who signs off on them?

168. How do you get the user to tell you what they want?

169. What is the risk associated with the technology?

170. What happens when requirements are wrong?

171. What facilities must be supported by the system?

2.5 Requirements Traceability Matrix: Policy Management Tools

172. Why do you manage scope?

173. What are the chronologies, contingencies, consequences, criteria?

174. Why use a WBS?

175. Do you have a clear understanding of all subcontracts in place?

176. What is the WBS?

177. Is there a requirements traceability process in place?

178. Will you use a Requirements Traceability Matrix?

179. Describe the process for approving requirements so they can be added to the traceability matrix and Policy Management Tools project work can be performed. Will the Policy Management Tools project requirements become approved in writing?

180. How small is small enough?

181. How do you manage scope?

182. What percentage of Policy Management Tools projects are producing traceability matrices between requirements and other work products?

183. How will it affect the stakeholders personally in career?

2.6 Project Scope Statement: Policy Management Tools

184. Were key Policy Management Tools project stakeholders brought into the Policy Management Tools project Plan?

185. Is there a Quality Assurance Plan documented and filed?

186. Is an issue management process documented and filed?

187. Is this process communicated to the customer and team members?

188. Will the Policy Management Tools project risks be managed according to the Policy Management Tools projects risk management process?

189. Have you been able to easily identify success criteria and create objective measurements for each of the Policy Management Tools project scopes goal statements?

190. Did your Policy Management Tools project ask for this?

191. Has a method and process for requirement tracking been developed?

192. Is the Policy Management Tools project manager qualified and experienced in Policy Management

Tools project management?

193. What actions will be taken to mitigate the risk?

194. Policy Management Tools project lead, team lead, solution architect?

195. Are there issues that could affect the existing requirements for the result, service, or product if the scope changes?

196. Is your organization structure appropriate for the Policy Management Tools projects size and complexity?

197. Is the Policy Management Tools project sponsor function identified and defined?

198. Have the reports to be produced, distributed, and filed been defined?

199. If you were to write a list of what should not be included in the scope statement, what are the things that you would recommend be described as out-of-scope?

200. Are there completion/verification criteria defined for each task producing an output?

201. Have the configuration management functions been assigned?

202. What are the defined meeting materials?

203. Will the risk documents be filed?

2.7 Assumption and Constraint Log: Policy Management Tools

204. Is this model reasonable?

205. Would known impacts serve as impediments?

206. What weaknesses do you have?

207. Is there a Steering Committee in place?

208. What if failure during recovery?

209. Have Policy Management Tools project management standards and procedures been established and documented?

210. Has the approach and development strategy of the Policy Management Tools project been defined, documented and accepted by the appropriate stakeholders?

211. Have all involved stakeholders and work groups committed to the Policy Management Tools project?

212. No superfluous information or marketing narrative?

213. What is positive about the current process?

214. Are there standards for code development?

215. What do you log?

216. Does a specific action and/or state that is known to violate security policy occur?

217. Are processes for release management of new development from coding and unit testing, to integration testing, to training, and production defined and followed?

218. Was the document/deliverable developed per the appropriate or required standards (for example, Institute of Electrical and Electronics Engineers standards)?

219. What threats might prevent you from getting there?

220. What do you audit?

221. Do you know what your customers expectations are regarding this process?

222. What to do at recovery?

223. Were the system requirements formally reviewed prior to initiating the design phase?

2.8 Work Breakdown Structure: Policy Management Tools

224. Why is it useful?

225. When does it have to be done?

226. Why would you develop a Work Breakdown Structure?

227. Who has to do it?

228. Is it a change in scope?

229. What is the probability of completing the Policy Management Tools project in less that xx days?

230. Can you make it?

231. How much detail?

232. What is the probability that the Policy Management Tools project duration will exceed xx weeks?

233. How far down?

234. How big is a work-package?

235. How many levels?

236. Where does it take place?

237. What has to be done?

238. When do you stop?

2.9 WBS Dictionary: Policy Management Tools

239. Are estimates developed by Policy Management Tools project personnel coordinated with the already stated responsible for overall management to determine whether required resources will be available according to revised planning?

240. Budgeted cost for work performed?

241. Changes in the current direct and Policy Management Tools projected base?

242. Are management actions taken to reduce indirect costs when there are significant adverse variances?

243. Time-phased control account budgets?

244. Are records maintained to show how undistributed budgets are controlled?

245. Does the contractors system provide for determination of price variance by comparing planned Vs actual commitments?

246. Detailed schedules which support control account and work package start and completion dates/events?

247. Is data disseminated to the contractors management timely, accurate, and usable?

248. Identify potential or actual overruns and underruns?

249. Do the lines of authority for incurring indirect costs correspond to the lines of responsibility for management control of the same components of costs?

250. Are all elements of indirect expense identified to overhead cost budgets of Policy Management Tools projections?

251. Is all budget available as management reserve identified and excluded from the performance measurement baseline?

252. Does the contractor use objective results, design reviews and tests to trace schedule performance?

253. What are you counting on?

254. What is the goal?

255. Are meaningful indicators identified for use in measuring the status of cost and schedule performance?

256. Are current work performance indicators and goals relatable to original goals as modified by contractual changes, replanning, and reprogramming actions?

257. Are direct or indirect cost adjustments being accomplished according to accounting procedures acceptable to us?

258. Are authorized changes being incorporated in a timely manner?

2.10 Schedule Management Plan: Policy Management Tools

259. Is there anything planned that does not need to be here?

260. Is current scope of the Policy Management Tools project substantially different than that originally defined?

261. Have Policy Management Tools project team accountabilities & responsibilities been clearly defined?

262. Were Policy Management Tools project team members involved in the development of activity & task decomposition?

263. Policy Management Tools project definition & scope?

264. Does all Policy Management Tools project documentation reside in a common repository for easy access?

265. Are the schedule estimates reasonable given the Policy Management Tools project?

266. Are changes in deliverable commitments agreed to by all affected groups & individuals?

267. Are all activities logically sequenced?

268. Is there an on-going process in place to monitor Policy Management Tools project risks?

269. Is there a formal set of procedures supporting Issues Management?

270. After initial schedule development, will the schedule be reviewed and validated by the Policy Management Tools project team?

271. Have stakeholder accountabilities & responsibilities been clearly defined?

272. Is the schedule vertically and horizontally traceable?

273. Is a process defined to measure the performance of the schedule management process itself?

274. Are Policy Management Tools project contact logs kept up to date?

275. Are actuals compared against estimates to analyze and correct variances?

276. What tools and techniques will be used to estimate activity resources?

277. Are assumptions being identified, recorded, analyzed, qualified and closed?

278. Are estimating assumptions and constraints captured?

2.11 Activity List: Policy Management Tools

279. What went wrong?

280. How detailed should a Policy Management Tools project get?

281. How difficult will it be to do specific activities on this Policy Management Tools project?

282. Can you determine the activity that must finish, before this activity can start?

283. What will be performed?

284. Should you include sub-activities?

285. What is the probability the Policy Management Tools project can be completed in xx weeks?

286. In what sequence?

287. Where will it be performed?

288. Who will perform the work?

289. What is the total time required to complete the Policy Management Tools project if no delays occur?

290. What are the critical bottleneck activities?

291. What is your organizations history in doing

similar activities?

292. What went well?

293. What is the LF and LS for each activity?

294. What did not go as well?

295. How much slack is available in the Policy Management Tools project?

2.12 Activity Attributes: Policy Management Tools

296. What is missing?

297. Activity: what is Missing?

298. Can more resources be added?

299. What conclusions/generalizations can you draw from this?

300. Would you consider either of corresponding activities an outlier?

301. Why?

302. How many resources do you need to complete the work scope within a limit of X number of days?

303. Is there a trend during the year?

304. Activity: fair or not fair?

305. Are the required resources available?

306. Activity: what is In the Bag?

307. How else could the items be grouped?

308. How do you manage time?

309. Resources to accomplish the work?

310. Are the required resources available or need to be acquired?

311. Which method produces the more accurate cost assignment?

2.13 Milestone List: Policy Management Tools

312. Insurmountable weaknesses?

313. What are your competitors vulnerabilities?

314. Can you derive how soon can the whole Policy Management Tools project finish?

315. Vital contracts and partners?

316. Information and research?

317. Describe the industry you are in and the market growth opportunities. What is the market for your technology, product or service?

318. Level of the Innovation?

319. Gaps in capabilities?

320. Calculate how long can activity be delayed?

321. How will the milestone be verified?

322. Effects on core activities, distraction?

323. Milestone pages should display the UserID of the person who added the milestone. Does a report or query exist that provides this audit information?

324. Who will manage the Policy Management Tools

project on a day-to-day basis?

325. Continuity, supply chain robustness?

326. How soon can the activity finish?

327. What background experience, skills, and strengths does the team bring to your organization?

2.14 Network Diagram: Policy Management Tools

328. What is the probability of completing the Policy Management Tools project in less that xx days?

329. What activities must occur simultaneously with this activity?

330. What is the completion time?

331. What job or jobs could run concurrently?

332. What controls the start and finish of a job?

333. Review the logical flow of the network diagram. Take a look at which activities you have first and then sequence the activities. Do they make sense?

334. What are the Major Administrative Issues?

335. What job or jobs follow it?

336. What must be completed before an activity can be started?

337. Planning: who, how long, what to do?

338. Where do you schedule uncertainty time?

339. What are the Key Success Factors?

340. If the Policy Management Tools project network

diagram cannot change and you have extra personnel resources, what is the BEST thing to do?

341. What can be done concurrently?

342. How confident can you be in your milestone dates and the delivery date?

343. Which type of network diagram allows you to depict four types of dependencies?

344. What to do and When?

2.15 Activity Resource Requirements: Policy Management Tools

345. When does monitoring begin?

346. Other support in specific areas?

347. Time for overtime?

348. What is the Work Plan Standard?

349. How many signatures do you require on a check and does this match what is in your policy and procedures?

350. How do you handle petty cash?

351. Why do you do that?

352. Anything else?

353. Are there unresolved issues that need to be addressed?

354. Organizational Applicability?

355. Do you use tools like decomposition and rolling-wave planning to produce the activity list and other outputs?

356. What are constraints that you might find during the Human Resource Planning process?

357. Which logical relationship does the PDM use most often?

2.16 Resource Breakdown Structure: Policy Management Tools

358. What is Policy Management Tools project communication management?

359. Which resources should be in the resource pool?

360. What is the number one predictor of a groups productivity?

361. Who is allowed to perform which functions?

362. Who delivers the information?

363. How should the information be delivered?

364. Any changes from stakeholders?

365. What is the purpose of assigning and documenting responsibility?

366. What is the primary purpose of the human resource plan?

367. Why is this important?

368. Goals for the Policy Management Tools project. What is each stakeholders desired outcome for the Policy Management Tools project?

369. What is the difference between % Complete and % work?

370. The list could probably go on, but, the thing that you would most like to know is, How long & How much?

371. What defines a successful Policy Management Tools project?

372. Who will be used as a Policy Management Tools project team member?

2.17 Activity Duration Estimates: Policy Management Tools

373. How can software assist in procuring goods and services?

374. Total slack can be calculated by which equations?

375. Is training acquired to enhance the skills, knowledge and capabilities of the Policy Management Tools project team?

376. How does the job market and current state of the economy affect human resource management?

377. Are time, scope, cost, and quality monitored throughout the Policy Management Tools project?

378. Are the causes of all variances identified?

379. What are two suggestions for ensuring adequate change control on Policy Management Tools projects that involve outside contracts?

380. Why time management?

381. Are Policy Management Tools project management tools and techniques consistently applied throughout all Policy Management Tools projects?

382. Does a process exist to formally recognize new Policy Management Tools projects?

383. How have experts such as Deming, Juran, Crosby, and Taguchi affected the quality movement and todays use of Six Sigma?

384. How does Policy Management Tools project management relate to other disciplines?

385. Do procedures exist that identify when and how human resources are introduced and removed from the Policy Management Tools project?

386. Will the new application be developed using existing hardware, software, and networks?

387. Account for the make-or-buy process and how to perform the financial calculations involved in the process. What are the main types of contracts if you do decide to outsource?

388. Find an example of a contract for information technology services. Analyze the key features of the contract. What type of contract was used and why?

389. Do stakeholders follow a procedure for formally accepting the Policy Management Tools project scope?

390. Why is activity definition the first process involved in Policy Management Tools project time management?

391. What are some general rules of thumb for deciding if cost variance, schedule variance, cost performance index, and schedule performance index numbers are good or bad?

392. Which suggestions do you find most useful?

2.18 Duration Estimating Worksheet: Policy Management Tools

393. What is an Average Policy Management Tools project?

394. Value pocket identification & quantification what are value pockets?

395. For other activities, how much delay can be tolerated?

396. Is this operation cost effective?

397. Why estimate costs?

398. Do any colleagues have experience with your organization and/or RFPs?

399. How can the Policy Management Tools project be displayed graphically to better visualize the activities?

400. What info is needed?

401. What is cost and Policy Management Tools project cost management?

402. What is your role?

403. What is the total time required to complete the Policy Management Tools project if no delays occur?

404. How should ongoing costs be monitored to try

to keep the Policy Management Tools project within budget?

405. Define the work as completely as possible. What work will be included in the Policy Management Tools project?

406. Does the Policy Management Tools project provide innovative ways for stakeholders to overcome obstacles or deliver better outcomes?

407. What work will be included in the Policy Management Tools project?

408. What utility impacts are there?

409. What questions do you have?

410. When do the individual activities need to start and finish?

411. Small or large Policy Management Tools project?

412. What is next?

2.19 Project Schedule: Policy Management Tools

413. What is risk management?

414. Are all remaining durations correct?

415. How do you know that youhave done this right?

416. Are quality inspections and review activities listed in the Policy Management Tools project schedule(s)?

417. Is the structure for tracking the Policy Management Tools project schedule well defined and assigned to a specific individual?

418. Your Policy Management Tools project management plan results in a Policy Management Tools project schedule that is too long. If the Policy Management Tools project network diagram cannot change and you have extra personnel resources, what is the BEST thing to do?

419. Eliminate unnecessary activities. Are there activities that came from a template or previous Policy Management Tools project that are not applicable on this phase of this Policy Management Tools project?

420. To what degree is do you feel the entire team was committed to the Policy Management Tools project schedule?

421. How effectively were issues able to be resolved without impacting the Policy Management Tools project Schedule or Budget?

422. Why is software Policy Management Tools project disaster so common?

423. How can you fix it?

424. Is infrastructure setup part of your Policy Management Tools project?

425. Is the Policy Management Tools project schedule available for all Policy Management Tools project team members to review?

426. Understand the constraints used in preparing the schedule. Are activities connected because logic dictates the order in which others occur?

427. Why or why not?

428. Are procedures defined by which the Policy Management Tools project schedule may be changed?

429. What is Policy Management Tools project management?

430. Have all Policy Management Tools project delays been adequately accounted for, communicated to all stakeholders and adjustments made in overall Policy Management Tools project schedule?

431. How closely did the initial Policy Management Tools project Schedule compare with the actual

schedule?

432. What documents, if any, will the subcontractor provide (eg Policy Management Tools project schedule, quality plan etc)?

2.20 Cost Management Plan: Policy Management Tools

433. Are schedule deliverables actually delivered?

434. Is the schedule updated on a periodic basis?

435. Resources – how will human resources be scheduled during each phase of the Policy Management Tools project?

436. Are milestone deliverables effectively tracked and compared to Policy Management Tools project plan?

437. Have process improvement efforts been completed before requirements efforts begin?

438. Are the Policy Management Tools project plans updated on a frequent basis?

439. What strengths do you have?

440. Designated small business reserve?

441. Is there a set of procedures defining the scope, procedures, and deliverables defining quality control?

442. What are the nine areas of expertise?

443. Are any non-compliance issues that exist due to State practices communicated to your organization?

444. Are risk triggers captured?

445. What would you do differently what did not work?

446. Has a capability assessment been conducted?

447. Are tasks tracked by hours?

448. Are the key elements of a Policy Management Tools project Charter present?

449. Were the budget estimates reasonable?

450. Contracting method – what contracting method is to be used for the contracts?

2.21 Activity Cost Estimates: Policy Management Tools

451. Why do you manage cost?

452. Which contract type places the most risk on the seller?

453. What is a Policy Management Tools project Management Plan?

454. One way to define activities is to consider how organization employees describe jobs to families and friends. You basically want to know, What do you do?

455. Are cost subtotals needed?

456. Was the consultant knowledgeable about the program?

457. What defines a successful Policy Management Tools project?

458. What happens if you cannot produce the documentation for the single audit?

459. Were the costs or charges reasonable?

460. How do you change activities?

461. What areas does the group agree are the biggest success on the Policy Management Tools project?

462. What makes a good activity description?

463. Does the estimator estimate by task or by person?

464. Review – what are some common errors in activities to avoid?

465. If you are asked to lower your estimate because the price is too high, what are your options?

466. Vac -variance at completion, how much over/under budget do you expect to be?

467. In which phase of the acquisition process cycle does source qualifications reside?

468. Who determines the quality and expertise of contractors?

469. What is the activity inventory?

2.22 Cost Estimating Worksheet: Policy Management Tools

470. Will the Policy Management Tools project collaborate with the local community and leverage resources?

471. Is the Policy Management Tools project responsive to community need?

472. Is it feasible to establish a control group arrangement?

473. Ask: are others positioned to know, are others credible, and will others cooperate?

474. What will others want?

475. Does the Policy Management Tools project provide innovative ways for stakeholders to overcome obstacles or deliver better outcomes?

476. What additional Policy Management Tools project(s) could be initiated as a result of this Policy Management Tools project?

477. Can a trend be established from historical performance data on the selected measure and are the criteria for using trend analysis or forecasting methods met?

478. What is the purpose of estimating?

479. What can be included?

480. Identify the timeframe necessary to monitor progress and collect data to determine how the selected measure has changed?

481. Who is best positioned to know and assist in identifying corresponding factors?

482. What costs are to be estimated?

483. How will the results be shared and to whom?

484. What happens to any remaining funds not used?

485. What is the estimated labor cost today based upon this information?

2.23 Cost Baseline: Policy Management Tools

486. Is there anything unique in this Policy Management Tools projects scope statement that will affect resources?

487. What is the most important thing to do next to make your Policy Management Tools project successful?

488. What can go wrong?

489. Policy Management Tools project goals -should others be reconsidered?

490. What is cost and Policy Management Tools project cost management?

491. What deliverables come first?

492. At which frequency ?

493. Has training and knowledge transfer of the operations organization been completed?

494. Does it impact schedule, cost, quality?

495. Is there anything you need from upper management in order to be successful?

496. Pcs for your new business. what would the life cycle costs be?

497. How concrete were original objectives?

498. Has the Policy Management Tools projected annual cost to operate and maintain the product(s) or service(s) been approved and funded?

499. On time?

500. Will the Policy Management Tools project fail if the change request is not executed?

501. Does a process exist for establishing a cost baseline to measure Policy Management Tools project performance?

502. Is the requested change request a result of changes in other Policy Management Tools project(s)?

503. Review your risk triggers -have your risks changed?

2.24 Quality Management Plan: Policy Management Tools

504. Is there a Quality Management Plan?

505. How are your organizations compensation and recognition approaches and the performance management system used to reinforce high performance?

506. Who else should be involved ?

507. What are your key performance measures/ indicators for tracking progress relative to your action plans?

508. How does your organization ensure the reliability, accuracy, timeliness, security and accessibility of data and information?

509. Are you meeting your customers expectations consistently?

510. Have adequate resources been provided by management to ensure Policy Management Tools project success?

511. When reporting to different audiences, do you vary the form or type of report?

512. How does your organization establish and maintain customer relationships?

513. What changes can you make that will result in improvement?

514. Modifications to the requirements?

515. Are you meeting the quality standards?

516. If it is out of compliance, should the process be amended or should the Plan be amended?

517. What type of in-house testing do you conduct?

518. What procedures are used to determine if you use, and the number of split, replicate or duplicate samples taken at a site?

519. Does a documented Policy Management Tools project organizational policy & plan (i.e. governance model) exist?

520. How many Policy Management Tools project staff does this specific process affect?

521. Why quality management?

2.25 Quality Metrics: Policy Management Tools

522. What forces exist that would cause them to change?

523. Is quality culture a competitive advantage?

524. Was material distributed on time?

525. How do you measure?

526. What can manufacturing professionals do to ensure quality is seen as an integral part of the entire product lifecycle?

527. Is there alignment within your organization on definitions?

528. Why is now the time for quality metrics?

529. Do you know how much profit a 10% decrease in waste would generate?

530. Are quality metrics defined?

531. What is the timeline to meet your goal?

532. How is it being measured?

533. What happens if you get an abnormal result?

534. Has trace of defects been initiated?

535. What is the benchmark?

536. What method of measurement do you use?

537. How can the effectiveness of each of the activities be measured?

538. Is the reporting frequency appropriate?

539. What does this tell us?

540. How do you calculate such metrics?

2.26 Process Improvement Plan: Policy Management Tools

541. What is the test-cycle concept?

542. Have the supporting tools been developed or acquired?

543. Who should prepare the process improvement action plan?

544. Does your process ensure quality?

545. What is quality and how will you ensure it?

546. Has a process guide to collect the data been developed?

547. Are there forms and procedures to collect and record the data?

548. What actions are needed to address the problems and achieve the goals?

549. If a process improvement framework is being used, which elements will help the problems and goals listed?

550. Are you making progress on the improvement framework?

551. Where do you focus?

552. Where do you want to be?

553. Purpose of goal: the motive is determined by asking, why do you want to achieve this goal?

554. What lessons have you learned so far?

555. Are you making progress on the goals?

556. Where are you now?

2.27 Responsibility Assignment Matrix: Policy Management Tools

557. How many people do you need?

558. Identify potential or actual budget-based and time-based schedule variances?

559. Ideas for developing soft skills at your organization?

560. Are overhead costs budgets established on a basis consistent with anticipated direct business base?

561. Changes in the direct base to which overhead costs are allocated?

562. Not any rs, as, or cs: if an identified role is only informed, should others be eliminated from the matrix?

563. What expertise is available in your department?

564. How cost benefit analysis?

565. All cwbs elements specified for external reporting?

566. Are estimates of costs at completion generated in a rational, consistent manner?

567. Who is the Policy Management Tools project

Manager?

568. Does the accounting system provide a basis for auditing records of direct costs chargeable to the contract?

569. What are the constraints?

570. Past experience – the person or the group worked at something similar in the past?

571. Performance to date and material commitment?

572. Cwbs elements to be subcontracted, with identification of subcontractors?

573. Actual cost of work performed?

2.28 Roles and Responsibilities: Policy Management Tools

574. Are Policy Management Tools project team roles and responsibilities identified and documented?

575. What should you do now to ensure that you are exceeding expectations and excelling in your current position?

576. Do the values and practices inherent in the culture of your organization foster or hinder the process?

577. Are Policy Management Tools project team roles and responsibilities identified and documented?

578. Are your budgets supportive of a culture of quality data?

579. Are the quality assurance functions and related roles and responsibilities clearly defined?

580. How is your work-life balance?

581. Is the data complete?

582. What should you do now to ensure that you are meeting all expectations of your current position?

583. Was the expectation clearly communicated?

584. Accountabilities: what are the roles and

responsibilities of individual team members?

585. Required skills, knowledge, experience?

586. What is working well within your organizations performance management system?

587. How well did the Policy Management Tools project Team understand the expectations of specific roles and responsibilities?

588. Is feedback clearly communicated and non-judgmental?

589. What expectations were met?

590. To decide whether to use a quality measurement, ask how will you know when it is achieved?

591. What areas would you highlight for changes or improvements?

2.29 Human Resource Management Plan: Policy Management Tools

592. Are there checklists created to determine if all quality processes are followed?

593. Are action items captured and managed?

594. Are the right people being attracted and retained to meet the future challenges?

595. Are key risk mitigation strategies added to the Policy Management Tools project schedule?

596. What were things that you need to improve?

597. Who are the people that make up your organization and whom create the success that your organization enjoys as a whole?

598. What are the Staffing Requirements?

599. Are Policy Management Tools project contact logs kept up to date?

600. Are the payment terms being followed?

601. Are risk oriented checklists used during risk identification?

602. Are all key components of a Quality Assurance Plan present?

603. Does the business case include how the Policy Management Tools project aligns with your organizations strategic goals & objectives?

604. Does the Policy Management Tools project have a Quality Culture?

605. Responsiveness to change and the resulting demands for different skills and abilities?

606. What were things that you did very well and want to do the same again on the next Policy Management Tools project?

607. Are the appropriate IT resources adequate to meet planned commitments?

608. Are staff skills known and available for each task?

2.30 Communications Management Plan: Policy Management Tools

609. How were corresponding initiatives successful?

610. Who were proponents/opponents?

611. How much time does it take to do it?

612. Are the stakeholders getting the information others need, are others consulted, are concerns addressed?

613. In your work, how much time is spent on stakeholder identification?

614. Who is involved as you identify stakeholders?

615. Is there an important stakeholder who is actively opposed and will not receive messages?

616. What data is going to be required?

617. Is the stakeholder role recognized by your organization?

618. Why manage stakeholders?

619. Why do you manage communications?

620. What approaches to you feel are the best ones to use?

621. What is the political influence?

622. What approaches do you use?

623. How often do you engage with stakeholders?

624. Will messages be directly related to the release strategy or phases of the Policy Management Tools project?

625. Do you feel a register helps?

626. Who did you turn to if you had questions?

627. Are others needed?

628. What are the interrelationships?

2.31 Risk Management Plan: Policy Management Tools

629. Are flexibility and reuse paramount?

630. What did not work so well?

631. Risk categories: what are the main categories of risks that should be addressed on this Policy Management Tools project?

632. Are the required plans included, such as nonstructural flood risk management plans?

633. Are you on schedule?

634. Have top software and customer managers formally committed to support the Policy Management Tools project?

635. Is the number of people on the Policy Management Tools project team adequate to do the job?

636. Are the reports useful and easy to read?

637. What are the chances the event will occur?

638. Monitoring -what factors can you track that will enable you to determine if the risk is becoming more or less likely?

639. What other risks are created by choosing an

avoidance strategy?

640. Do you have a consistent repeatable process that is actually used?

641. What risks are necessary to achieve success?

642. Which risks should get the attention?

643. Was an original risk assessment/risk management plan completed?

644. How is risk identification performed?

645. Is there anything you would now do differently on your Policy Management Tools project based on this experience?

646. What would you do differently?

647. Is the necessary data being captured and is it complete and accurate?

2.32 Risk Register: Policy Management Tools

648. Can the likelihood and impact of failing to achieve corresponding recommendations and action plans be assessed?

649. What is the appropriate level of risk management for this Policy Management Tools project?

650. Does the evidence highlight any areas to advance opportunities or foster good relations. If yes what steps will be taken?

651. Recovery actions - planned actions taken once a risk has occurred to allow you to move on. What should you do after?

652. What action, if any, has been taken to respond to the risk?

653. Manageability – have mitigations to the risk been identified?

654. Assume the risk event or situation happens, what would the impact be?

655. Methodology: how will risk management be performed on this Policy Management Tools project?

656. When is it going to be done?

657. Having taken action, how did the responses

effect change, and where is the Policy Management Tools project now?

658. Are corrective measures implemented as planned?

659. Severity Prediction?

660. How are risks graded?

661. Why would you develop a risk register?

662. Are your objectives at risk?

663. Budget and schedule: what are the estimated costs and schedules for performing risk-related activities?

664. What can be done about it?

665. What is your current and future risk profile?

666. What evidence do you have to justify the likelihood score of the risk (audit, incident report, claim, complaints, inspection, internal review)?

2.33 Probability and Impact Assessment: Policy Management Tools

667. Are enough people available?

668. Assuming that you have identified a number of risks in the Policy Management Tools project, how would you prioritize them?

669. What will be the impact or consequence if the risk occurs?

670. Do the people have the right combinations of skills?

671. What will be the likely political environment during the life of the Policy Management Tools project?

672. Is the present organizational structure for handling the Policy Management Tools project sufficient?

673. Can it be enlarged by drawing people from other areas of your organization?

674. Who has experience with this?

675. Does the software engineering team have the right mix of skills?

676. Is the Policy Management Tools project cutting

across the entire organization?

677. What would be the effect of slippage?

678. What should be the gestation period for the Policy Management Tools project with specific technology?

679. How would you suggest monitoring for risk transition indicators?

680. Do benefits and chances of success outweigh potential damage if success is not attained?

681. What is the probability of the risk occurring?

682. How are the local factors going to affect the absorption?

2.34 Probability and Impact Matrix: Policy Management Tools

683. What changes in the regulation are forthcoming?

684. Can the Policy Management Tools project proceed without assuming the risk?

685. What action would you take to the identified risks in the Policy Management Tools project?

686. What should be the level of difficulty in handling the technology?

687. What are the uncertainties associated with the technology selected for the Policy Management Tools project?

688. Which role do you have in the Policy Management Tools project?

689. How would you assess the risk management process in the Policy Management Tools project?

690. What is the likelihood of a breakthrough?

691. What can you do about it?

692. Pay attention to the quality of the plans: is the content complete, or does it seem to be lacking detail?

693. Have top software and customer managers

formally committed to support the Policy Management Tools project?

694. Is a software Policy Management Tools project management tool available?

695. How is the risk management process used in practice?

696. Do requirements demand the use of new analysis, design, or testing methods?

697. What are the channels available for distribution to the customer?

698. Are the risk data timely and relevant?

699. What things are likely to change?

700. What can you use the analyzed risks for?

701. What are the current demands of the customer?

2.35 Risk Data Sheet: Policy Management Tools

702. Whom do you serve (customers)?

703. What will be the consequences if the risk happens?

704. What are the main opportunities available to you that you should grab while you can?

705. What are you trying to achieve (Objectives)?

706. What was measured?

707. What actions can be taken to eliminate or remove risk?

708. Has a sensitivity analysis been carried out?

709. Risk of what?

710. What are your core values?

711. What are you weak at and therefore need to do better?

712. What do you know?

713. How can it happen?

714. What are you here for (Mission)?

715. Who has a vested interest in how you perform as your organization (our stakeholders)?

716. What do people affected think about the need for, and practicality of preventive measures?

717. Is the data sufficiently specified in terms of the type of failure being analyzed, and its frequency or probability?

718. What is the likelihood of it happening?

719. What are the main threats to your existence?

720. What will be the consequences if it happens?

2.36 Procurement Management Plan: Policy Management Tools

721. Have reserves been created to address risks?

722. How will you coordinate Procurement with aspects of the Policy Management Tools project?

723. Is the current scope of the Policy Management Tools project substantially different than that originally defined?

724. Are quality inspections and review activities listed in the Policy Management Tools project schedule(s)?

725. Are status reports received per the Policy Management Tools project Plan?

726. Are key risk mitigation strategies added to the Policy Management Tools project schedule?

727. Have external dependencies been captured in the schedule?

728. Are post milestone Policy Management Tools project reviews (PMPR) conducted with your organization at least once a year?

729. Has a Policy Management Tools project Communications Plan been developed?

730. Why do you do it?

731. What is a Policy Management Tools project Management Plan?

732. Financial capacity; does the seller have, or can the seller reasonably be expected to obtain, the financial resources needed?

733. Is there any form of automated support for Issues Management?

734. Has a resource management plan been created?

735. Is there an on-going process in place to monitor Policy Management Tools project risks?

736. Do Policy Management Tools project managers participating in the Policy Management Tools project know the Policy Management Tools projects true status first hand?

2.37 Source Selection Criteria: Policy Management Tools

737. What is the role of counsel in the procurement process?

738. Is experience evaluated?

739. Are there any common areas of weaknesses or deficiencies in the proposals in the competitive range?

740. What common questions or problems are associated with debriefings?

741. How will you evaluate offerors proposals?

742. What is the last item a Policy Management Tools project manager must do to finalize Policy Management Tools project close-out?

743. How are oral presentations documented?

744. Do you consider all weaknesses, significant weaknesses, and deficiencies?

745. What is the basis of an estimate and what assumptions were made?

746. Is there collaboration among your evaluators?

747. Are types/quantities of material, facilities appropriate?

748. What should preproposal conferences accomplish?

749. What will you use to capture evaluation and subsequent documentation?

750. What are the most common types of rating systems?

751. Can you reasonably estimate total organization requirements for the coming year?

752. In the technical/management area, what criteria do you use to determine the final evaluation ratings?

753. What should be considered?

754. What documentation is needed for a tradeoff decision?

755. What are open book debriefings?

2.38 Stakeholder Management Plan: Policy Management Tools

756. Have Policy Management Tools project management standards and procedures been established and documented?

757. Is quality monitored from the perspective of the customers needs and expectations?

758. What has to be purchased?

759. Are the schedule estimates reasonable given the Policy Management Tools project?

760. Has the scope management document been updated and distributed to help prevent scope creep?

761. Are there ways to reduce the time it takes to get something approved?

762. Have the procedures for identifying budget variances been followed?

763. Does the business case include how the Policy Management Tools project aligns with your organizations strategic goals & objectives?

764. Is stakeholder involvement adequate?

765. How, to whom and how frequently will Risk status be reported?

766. Is there an onboarding process in place?

767. What information should be collected?

768. What proven methodologies and standards will be used to ensure that materials, products, processes and services are fit for purpose?

769. Is Policy Management Tools project status reviewed with the steering and executive teams at appropriate intervals?

770. Who is gathering information?

771. What is the drawback in using qualitative Policy Management Tools project selection techniques?

772. What is the general purpose in defining responsibilities of the already stated affiliated with the Policy Management Tools project?

773. What are the advantages and disadvantages of using external contracted resources?

774. Has the Policy Management Tools project scope been baselined?

2.39 Change Management Plan: Policy Management Tools

775. Who is the target audience of the piece of information?

776. When developing your communication plan do you address : When should the given message be communicated?

777. What are the key change management success metrics?

778. Will all field readiness criteria have been practically met prior to training roll-out?

779. What work practices will be affected?

780. What prerequisite knowledge do corresponding groups need?

781. When to start change management?

782. Has the priority for this Policy Management Tools project been set by the Business Unit Management Team?

783. What are the dependencies?

784. Is there an adequate supply of people for the new roles?

785. What is the most positive interpretation it can

receive?

786. Has a training need analysis been carried out?

787. Readiness -what is a successful end state?

788. What are you trying to achieve as a result of communication?

789. Who might be able to help you the most?

790. Who will be the change levers?

791. Will you need new processes?

792. Impact of systems implementation on organization change?

3.0 Executing Process Group: Policy Management Tools

793. How will you avoid scope creep?

794. Specific - is the objective clear in terms of what, how, when, and where the situation will be changed?

795. Measurable - are the targets measurable?

796. Based on your Policy Management Tools project communication management plan, what worked well?

797. What does it mean to take a systems view of a Policy Management Tools project?

798. What were things that you did very well and want to do the same again on the next Policy Management Tools project?

799. Why is it important to determine activity sequencing on Policy Management Tools projects?

800. On which process should team members spend the most time?

801. Does the case present a realistic scenario?

802. What are the main parts of the scope statement?

803. Do Policy Management Tools project managers understand your organizational context for Policy

Management Tools projects?

804. When do you share the scorecard with managers?

805. Why do you need a good WBS to use Policy Management Tools project management software?

806. What are the main processes included in Policy Management Tools project quality management?

807. What good practices or successful experiences or transferable examples have been identified?

808. What are deliverables of your Policy Management Tools project?

809. Is the schedule for the set products being met?

810. If action is called for, what form should it take?

811. What is the shortest possible time it will take to complete this Policy Management Tools project?

3.1 Team Member Status Report: Policy Management Tools

812. Why is it to be done?

813. Are the products of your organizations Policy Management Tools projects meeting customers objectives?

814. How does this product, good, or service meet the needs of the Policy Management Tools project and your organization as a whole?

815. Does the product, good, or service already exist within your organization?

816. Do you have an Enterprise Policy Management Tools project Management Office (EPMO)?

817. What is to be done?

818. The problem with Reward & Recognition Programs is that the truly deserving people all too often get left out. How can you make it practical?

819. How it is to be done?

820. Are the attitudes of staff regarding Policy Management Tools project work improving?

821. How much risk is involved?

822. Will the staff do training or is that done by a third

party?

823. Does every department have to have a Policy Management Tools project Manager on staff?

824. Are your organizations Policy Management Tools projects more successful over time?

825. When a teams productivity and success depend on collaboration and the efficient flow of information, what generally fails them?

826. Does your organization have the means (staff, money, contract, etc.) to produce or to acquire the product, good, or service?

827. Is there evidence that staff is taking a more professional approach toward management of your organizations Policy Management Tools projects?

828. What specific interest groups do you have in place?

829. How will resource planning be done?

830. How can you make it practical?

3.2 Change Request: Policy Management Tools

831. Who is communicating the change?

832. How do you get changes (code) out in a timely manner?

833. What type of changes does change control take into account?

834. Are there requirements attributes that are strongly related to the occurrence of defects and failures?

835. Does the schedule include Policy Management Tools project management time and change request analysis time?

836. Are there requirements attributes that can discriminate between high and low reliability?

837. Will this change conflict with other requirements changes (e.g., lead to conflicting operational scenarios)?

838. How is quality being addressed on the Policy Management Tools project?

839. Who has responsibility for approving and ranking changes?

840. Who can suggest changes?

841. What should be regulated in a change control operating instruction?

842. Are you implementing itil processes?

843. Will new change requests be acknowledged in a timely manner?

844. Will the change use memory to the extent that other functions will be not have sufficient memory to operate effectively?

845. Are there requirements attributes that are strongly related to the complexity and size?

846. What is the purpose of change control?

847. Who is included in the change control team?

848. What is the relationship between requirements attributes and reliability?

849. What is a Change Request Form?

850. Change request coordination ?

3.3 Change Log: Policy Management Tools

851. Is this a mandatory replacement?

852. How does this change affect the timeline of the schedule?

853. How does this relate to the standards developed for specific business processes?

854. Is the change request open, closed or pending?

855. Does the suggested change request seem to represent a necessary enhancement to the product?

856. Do the described changes impact on the integrity or security of the system?

857. Is the change backward compatible without limitations?

858. When was the request approved?

859. Does the suggested change request represent a desired enhancement to the products functionality?

860. Who initiated the change request?

861. Is the requested change request a result of changes in other Policy Management Tools project(s)?

862. Is the change request within Policy Management

Tools project scope?

863. Is the submitted change a new change or a modification of a previously approved change?

864. When was the request submitted?

865. How does this change affect scope?

866. Where do changes come from?

867. Should a more thorough impact analysis be conducted?

868. Will the Policy Management Tools project fail if the change request is not executed?

3.4 Decision Log: Policy Management Tools

869. What eDiscovery problem or issue did your organization set out to fix or make better?

870. Adversarial environment. is your opponent open to a non-traditional workflow, or will it likely challenge anything you do?

871. What are the cost implications?

872. With whom was the decision shared or considered?

873. How does the use a Decision Support System influence the strategies/tactics or costs?

874. Who will be given a copy of this document and where will it be kept?

875. What is the line where eDiscovery ends and document review begins?

876. What was the rationale for the decision?

877. How do you know when you are achieving it?

878. What is the average size of your matters in an applicable measurement?

879. Decision-making process; how will the team make decisions?

880. Behaviors; what are guidelines that the team has identified that will assist them with getting the most out of team meetings?

881. How effective is maintaining the log at facilitating organizational learning?

882. What is your overall strategy for quality control / quality assurance procedures?

883. How consolidated and comprehensive a story can you tell by capturing currently available incident data in a central location and through a log of key decisions during an incident?

884. What makes you different or better than others companies selling the same thing?

885. It becomes critical to track and periodically revisit both operational effectiveness; Are you noticing all that you need to, and are you interpreting what you see effectively?

886. Do strategies and tactics aimed at less than full control reduce the costs of management or simply shift the cost burden?

887. Which variables make a critical difference?

888. Linked to original objective?

3.5 Quality Audit: Policy Management Tools

889. Are training programs documented?

890. How does your organization know that its systems for communicating with and among staff are appropriately effective and constructive?

891. How are you auditing your organizations compliance with regulations?

892. How does your organization know that its relationships with industry and employers are appropriately effective and constructive?

893. Are measuring and test equipment that have been placed out of service suitably identified and excluded from use in any device reconditioning operation?

894. How does your organization know that the range and quality of its accommodation, catering and transportation services are appropriately effective and constructive?

895. How does your organization know that its processes for managing severance are appropriately effective, constructive and fair?

896. How does your organization know that its advisory services are appropriately effective and constructive?

897. Are adequate and conveniently located toilet facilities available for use by the employees?

898. Can your organization demonstrate exactly how and why results were achieved?

899. How does your organization know that its system for examining work done is appropriately effective and constructive?

900. Is your organizational structure a help or a hindrance to deployment?

901. How do staff know if they are doing a good job?

902. How does your organization know that its risk management system is appropriately effective and constructive?

903. How does your organization know that the research supervision provided to its staff is appropriately effective and constructive?

904. How does your organization know that its general support services planning and management systems are appropriately effective and constructive?

905. What has changed/improved as a result of the review processes?

906. Is progress against the intentions measurable?

907. How does your organization know that its system for recruiting the best staff possible are appropriately effective and constructive?

908. Is there a written corporate quality policy?

3.6 Team Directory: Policy Management Tools

909. Process decisions: are there any statutory or regulatory issues relevant to the timely execution of work?

910. Why is the work necessary?

911. Days from the time the issue is identified?

912. Process decisions: do invoice amounts match accepted work in place?

913. Process decisions: are contractors adequately prosecuting the work?

914. How and in what format should information be presented?

915. When does information need to be distributed?

916. Process decisions: do job conditions warrant additional actions to collect job information and document on-site activity?

917. Who are the Team Members?

918. Process decisions: are all start-up, turn over and close out requirements of the contract satisfied?

919. Who are your stakeholders (customers, sponsors, end users, team members)?

920. Who will report Policy Management Tools project status to all stakeholders?

921. Is construction on schedule?

922. Where should the information be distributed?

923. What needs to be communicated?

924. Contract requirements complied with?

925. Decisions: is the most suitable form of contract being used?

926. Who should receive information (all stakeholders)?

927. Decisions: what could be done better to improve the quality of the constructed product?

3.7 Team Operating Agreement: Policy Management Tools

928. Confidentiality: how will confidential information be handled?

929. Has the appropriate access to relevant data and analysis capability been granted?

930. Do you listen for voice tone and word choice to understand the meaning behind words?

931. Methodologies: how will key team processes be implemented, such as training, research, work deliverable production, review and approval processes, knowledge management, and meeting procedures?

932. What are the boundaries (organizational or geographic) within which you operate?

933. Do team members reside in more than two countries?

934. What is your unique contribution to your organization?

935. Do you call or email participants to ensure understanding, follow-through and commitment to the meeting outcomes?

936. Are there influences outside the team that may affect performance, and if so, have you identified and

addressed them?

937. What are some potential sources of conflict among team members?

938. How does teaming fit in with overall organizational goals and meet organizational needs?

939. Must your members collaborate successfully to complete Policy Management Tools projects?

940. Are there more than two native languages represented by your team?

941. What resources can be provided for the team in terms of equipment, space, time for training, protected time and space for meetings, and travel allowances?

942. Do you solicit member feedback about meetings and what would make them better?

943. Did you draft the meeting agenda?

944. What is teaming?

945. Did you recap the meeting purpose, time, and expectations?

946. Reimbursements: how will the team members be reimbursed for expenses and time commitments?

3.8 Team Performance Assessment: Policy Management Tools

947. To what degree do the goals specify concrete team work products?

948. To what degree do team members understand one anothers roles and skills?

949. To what degree will the team adopt a concrete, clearly understood, and agreed-upon approach that will result in achievement of the teams goals?

950. How do you manage human resources?

951. To what degree are the goals realistic?

952. To what degree are the teams goals and objectives clear, simple, and measurable?

953. What makes opportunities more or less obvious?

954. How do you encourage members to learn from each other?

955. To what degree does the teams work approach provide opportunity for members to engage in open interaction?

956. To what degree do team members articulate the teams work approach?

957. When does the medium matter?

958. What do you think is the most constructive thing that could be done now to resolve considerations and disputes about method variance?

959. How much interpersonal friction is there in your team?

960. To what degree is there a sense that only the team can succeed?

961. To what degree are the skill areas critical to team performance present?

962. To what degree can team members vigorously define the teams purpose in considerations with others who are not part of the functioning team?

963. If you have received criticism from reviewers that your work suffered from method variance, what was the circumstance?

964. To what degree can all members engage in open and interactive considerations?

965. If you are worried about method variance before you collect data, what sort of design elements might you include to reduce or eliminate the threat of method variance?

966. Delaying market entry: how long is too long?

3.9 Team Member Performance Assessment: Policy Management Tools

967. What happens if a team member receives a Rating of Unsatisfactory?

968. How is the timing of assessments organized (e.g., pre/post-test, single point during training, multiple reassessment during training)?

969. How do you work together to improve teaching and learning?

970. What are the staffs preferences for training on technology-based platforms?

971. Does the rater (supervisor) have to wait for the interim or final performance assessment review to tell an employee that the employees performance is unsatisfactory?

972. What are best practices for delivering and developing training evaluations to maximize the benefits of leveraging emerging technologies?

973. What tools are available to determine whether all contract functional and compliance areas of performance objectives, measures, and incentives have been met?

974. Why do performance reviews?

975. Does the rater (supervisor) have the authority or responsibility to tell an employee that the employees performance is unsatisfactory?

976. Which training platform formats (i.e., mobile, virtual, videogame-based) were implemented in your effort(s)?

977. For what period of time is a member rated?

978. What types of learning are targeted (e.g., cognitive, affective, psychomotor, procedural)?

979. Who receives a benchmark visit?

980. To what degree is the team cognizant of small wins to be celebrated along the way?

981. What is the target group for instruction (e.g., individual and collective or small team instruction)?

982. To what degree are the goals ambitious?

983. Should a ratee get a copy of all the raters documents about the employees performance?

984. Is there reluctance to join a team?

985. What is collaboration?

986. What evaluation results do you have?

3.10 Issue Log: Policy Management Tools

987. Which stakeholders are thought leaders, influences, or early adopters?

988. How is this initiative related to other portfolios, programs, or Policy Management Tools projects?

989. Are there common objectives between the team and the stakeholder?

990. How were past initiatives successful?

991. Are they needed?

992. Who reported the issue?

993. In classifying stakeholders, which approach to do so are you using?

994. Do you often overlook a key stakeholder or stakeholder group?

995. Which team member will work with each stakeholder?

996. Who is the stakeholder?

997. What is the impact on the Business Case?

998. How do you reply to this question; you am new here and managing this major program. How do you

suggest you build your network?

999. What effort will a change need?

1000. Are the Policy Management Tools project issues uniquely identified, including to which product they refer?

1001. What date was the issue resolved?

1002. Where do team members get information?

4.0 Monitoring and Controlling Process Group: Policy Management Tools

1003. How should needs be met?

1004. Who are the Policy Management Tools project stakeholders?

1005. Did the Policy Management Tools project team have enough people to execute the Policy Management Tools project plan?

1006. Change, where should you look for problems?

1007. How to ensure validity, quality and consistency?

1008. Is there sufficient time allotted between the general system design and the detailed system design phases?

1009. Did the Policy Management Tools project team have the right skills?

1010. Is there sufficient funding available for this?

1011. How well did you do?

1012. What kinds of things in particular are you looking for data on?

1013. Just how important is your work to the overall success of the Policy Management Tools project?

1014. Is it what was agreed upon?

1015. How is agile portfolio management done?

1016. What do they need to know about the Policy Management Tools project?

1017. Propriety: who needs to be involved in the evaluation to be ethical?

4.1 Project Performance Report: Policy Management Tools

1018. To what degree does the teams purpose constitute a broader, deeper aspiration than just accomplishing short-term goals?

1019. To what degree are the members clear on what they are individually responsible for and what they are jointly responsible for?

1020. To what degree are the demands of the task compatible with and converge with the mission and functions of the formal organization?

1021. To what degree will each member have the opportunity to advance his or her professional skills in all three of the above categories while contributing to the accomplishment of the teams purpose and goals?

1022. To what degree is the information network consistent with the structure of the formal organization?

1023. To what degree do all members feel responsible for all agreed-upon measures?

1024. To what degree is there centralized control of information sharing?

1025. To what degree do the structures of the formal organization motivate taskrelevant behavior and facilitate task completion?

1026. What degree are the relative importance and priority of the goals clear to all team members?

1027. To what degree will new and supplemental skills be introduced as the need is recognized?

1028. To what degree does the information network communicate information relevant to the task?

1029. To what degree can the team measure progress against specific goals?

1030. How can Policy Management Tools project sustainability be maintained?

1031. To what degree does the informal organization make use of individual resources and meet individual needs?

1032. To what degree does the team possess adequate membership to achieve its ends?

4.2 Variance Analysis: Policy Management Tools

1033. Is work progressively subdivided into detailed work packages as requirements are defined?

1034. Can the contractor substantiate work package and planning package budgets?

1035. How does the use of a single conversion element (rather than the traditional labor and overhead elements) affect standard costing?

1036. Are procedures for variance analysis documented and consistently applied at the control account level and selected WBS and organizational levels at least monthly as a routine task?

1037. Contract line items and end items?

1038. Do work packages consist of discrete tasks which are adequately described?

1039. What is the budgeted cost for work scheduled?

1040. Favorable or unfavorable variance?

1041. Wbs elements contractually specified for reporting of status to your organization (lowest level only)?

1042. How does the monthly budget compare to the actual experience?

1043. Are the wbs and organizational levels for application of the Policy Management Tools projected overhead costs identified?

1044. Do the rates and prices remain constant throughout the year?

1045. Historical experience?

1046. What causes selling price variance?

1047. Are all authorized tasks assigned to identified organizational elements?

1048. What business event caused the fluctuation?

1049. What is the total budget for the Policy Management Tools project (including estimates for authorized and unpriced work)?

1050. How do you verify authorization to proceed with all authorized work?

4.3 Earned Value Status: Policy Management Tools

1051. How much is it going to cost by the finish?

1052. Where are your problem areas?

1053. When is it going to finish?

1054. Earned value can be used in almost any Policy Management Tools project situation and in almost any Policy Management Tools project environment. it may be used on large Policy Management Tools projects, medium sized Policy Management Tools projects, tiny Policy Management Tools projects (in cut-down form), complex and simple Policy Management Tools projects and in any market sector. some people, of course, know all about earned value, they have used it for years - but perhaps not as effectively as they could have?

1055. Verification is a process of ensuring that the developed system satisfies the stakeholders agreements and specifications; Are you building the product right? What do you verify?

1056. What is the unit of forecast value?

1057. Are you hitting your Policy Management Tools projects targets?

1058. If earned value management (EVM) is so good in determining the true status of a Policy Management

Tools project and Policy Management Tools project its completion, why is it that hardly any one uses it in information systems related Policy Management Tools projects?

1059. Where is evidence-based earned value in your organization reported?

1060. Validation is a process of ensuring that the developed system will actually achieve the stakeholders desired outcomes; Are you building the right product? What do you validate?

1061. How does this compare with other Policy Management Tools projects?

4.4 Risk Audit: Policy Management Tools

1062. To what extent are auditors effective at linking business risks and management assertions?

1063. Is there (or should there be) some impact on the process of setting materiality when the auditor more effectively identifies higher risk areas of the financial statements?

1064. What are the risks that could stop you from achieving your objectives?

1065. Do end-users have realistic expectations?

1066. What are the legal implications of not identifying a complete universe of business risks?

1067. Is the technology to be built new to your organization?

1068. Does the implementation method matter?

1069. What are the boundaries of the auditors responsibility for policing management fidelity?

1070. Improving fraud detection: do auditors react to abnormal inconsistencies between financial and non-financial measures?

1071. Does your organization have a register of insurance policies detailing all current insurance policies?

1072. What are the costs associated with late delivery or a defective product?

1073. How do you compare to other jurisdictions when managing the risk of ....?

1074. Have all possible risks/hazards been identified (including injury to staff, damage to equipment, impact on others in the community)?

1075. Who audits the auditor?

1076. Is an annual audit required and conducted of your financial records?

1077. How can the strategy fail/achieved?

1078. Does your organization have a process for meeting its ongoing taxation obligations?

1079. Have top software and customer managers formally committed to support the Policy Management Tools project?

1080. Do all coaches/instructors/leaders have appropriate and current accreditation?

4.5 Contractor Status Report: Policy Management Tools

1081. How does the proposed individual meet each requirement?

1082. Describe how often regular updates are made to the proposed solution. Are corresponding regular updates included in the standard maintenance plan?

1083. How long have you been using the services?

1084. What process manages the contracts?

1085. Who can list a Policy Management Tools project as organization experience, your organization or a previous employee of your organization?

1086. How is risk transferred?

1087. What was the overall budget or estimated cost?

1088. What was the actual budget or estimated cost for your organizations services?

1089. What are the minimum and optimal bandwidth requirements for the proposed solution?

1090. What was the budget or estimated cost for your organizations services?

1091. Are there contractual transfer concerns?

1092. What is the average response time for answering a support call?

1093. If applicable; describe your standard schedule for new software version releases. Are new software version releases included in the standard maintenance plan?

1094. What was the final actual cost?

4.6 Formal Acceptance: Policy Management Tools

1095. Was the sponsor/customer satisfied?

1096. What are the requirements against which to test, Who will execute?

1097. Was the Policy Management Tools project managed well?

1098. Is formal acceptance of the Policy Management Tools project product documented and distributed?

1099. Do you buy-in installation services?

1100. Do you buy pre-configured systems or build your own configuration?

1101. What can you do better next time?

1102. Have all comments been addressed?

1103. Was the Policy Management Tools project work done on time, within budget, and according to specification?

1104. What function(s) does it fill or meet?

1105. Was the client satisfied with the Policy Management Tools project results?

1106. Who supplies data?

1107. Was business value realized?

1108. Do you perform formal acceptance or burn-in tests?

1109. Did the Policy Management Tools project manager and team act in a professional and ethical manner?

1110. What is the Acceptance Management Process?

1111. General estimate of the costs and times to complete the Policy Management Tools project?

1112. Who would use it?

1113. Does it do what Policy Management Tools project team said it would?

1114. What features, practices, and processes proved to be strengths or weaknesses?

5.0 Closing Process Group: Policy Management Tools

1115. When will the Policy Management Tools project be done?

1116. What level of risk does the proposed budget represent to the Policy Management Tools project?

1117. Contingency planning. if a risk event occurs, what will you do?

1118. What business situation is being addressed?

1119. Mitigate. what will you do to minimize the impact should a risk event occur?

1120. Were cost budgets met?

1121. Is the Policy Management Tools project funded?

1122. Are there funding or time constraints?

1123. What were the actual outcomes?

1124. What will you do to minimize the impact should a risk event occur?

1125. Is there a clear cause and effect between the activity and the lesson learned?

1126. What is the risk of failure to your organization?

1127. Did the Policy Management Tools project management methodology work?

1128. Was the user/client satisfied with the end product?

1129. Is this a follow-on to a previous Policy Management Tools project?

1130. What could have been improved?

5.1 Procurement Audit: Policy Management Tools

1131. Is your organization transparent about winning bids and prices?

1132. Are the pages of the minutes book press pre-numbered?

1133. Is the opportunity properly published?

1134. Are there regular accounting reconciliations of contract payments, transactions and inventory?

1135. Where required, did candidates give evidence of complying with required environmental management standards?

1136. Are required quality and service standards set?

1137. Where funding is being arranged by borrowings, do corresponding have the necessary approval and legal authority?

1138. Is there a policy on purchasing from users of organization products?

1139. When competitive dialogue was used, did the contracting authority provide sufficient justification for the use of this procedure and was the contract actually particularly complex?

1140. Are behaviour modification applied to change

procurement of goods and services if procurement is not functioning properly?

1141. Are all checks pre-numbered?

1142. Is there a policy on making purchases locally where possible?

1143. Are internal control mechanisms performed before payments?

1144. Was the tender clearly and properly specified, including evaluation criteria and knowing about the market and therefore not over-prescriptive and receptive to innovation?

1145. Was the outcome of the award process properly reached and communicated?

1146. Is it clear which procurement procedure your organization has opted for?

1147. Are reports based on sound data available to the already stated responsible for monitoring the performance of contracts?

1148. Is there no evidence of any individual on the evaluation panel being biased?

1149. Has your organization clearly defined the award criteria?

1150. Are incentives to deliver on time and in quantity properly specified?

5.2 Contract Close-Out: Policy Management Tools

1151. How is the contracting office notified of the automatic contract close-out?

1152. Change in circumstances?

1153. How does it work?

1154. Parties: who is involved?

1155. Have all contracts been completed?

1156. Are the signers the authorized officials?

1157. Change in attitude or behavior?

1158. Was the contract type appropriate?

1159. Have all acceptance criteria been met prior to final payment to contractors?

1160. Why Outsource?

1161. What is capture management?

1162. How/when used ?

1163. Was the contract sufficiently clear so as not to result in numerous disputes and misunderstandings?

1164. Was the contract complete without requiring

numerous changes and revisions?

1165. Parties: Authorized?

1166. Have all contracts been closed?

1167. Has each contract been audited to verify acceptance and delivery?

1168. Change in knowledge?

1169. Have all contract records been included in the Policy Management Tools project archives?

1170. What happens to the recipient of services?

5.3 Project or Phase Close-Out: Policy Management Tools

1171. Were the outcomes different from the already stated planned?

1172. Which changes might a stakeholder be required to make as a result of the Policy Management Tools project?

1173. What information is each stakeholder group interested in?

1174. Can the lesson learned be replicated?

1175. In addition to assessing whether the Policy Management Tools project was successful, it is equally critical to analyze why it was or was not fully successful. Are you including this?

1176. Were risks identified and mitigated?

1177. What was expected from each stakeholder?

1178. What are the marketing communication needs for each stakeholder?

1179. Planned completion date?

1180. Did the delivered product meet the specified requirements and goals of the Policy Management Tools project?

1181. Who controlled key decisions that were made?

1182. Does the lesson describe a function that would be done differently the next time?

1183. Was the schedule met?

1184. Were messages directly related to the release strategy or phases of the Policy Management Tools project?

1185. What was learned?

1186. Complete yes or no?

1187. What can you do better next time, and what specific actions can you take to improve?

5.4 Lessons Learned: Policy Management Tools

1188. What would you change?

1189. Is there any way in which you think your development process hampered this Policy Management Tools project?

1190. How smooth do you feel Integration has been?

1191. Was any formal risk assessment carried out at the start of the Policy Management Tools project, and was this followed up during the Policy Management Tools project?

1192. What is the frequency of group communications?

1193. Did the Policy Management Tools project management methodology work?

1194. How adequately involved did you feel in Policy Management Tools project decisions?

1195. Were any strategies or activities unsuccessful?

1196. What are the internal fiscal constraints?

1197. How much of your time was spent on other than this Policy Management Tools project?

1198. What is below the surface?

1199. How actively and meaningfully were stakeholders involved in the Policy Management Tools project?

1200. Is the lesson based on actual Policy Management Tools project experience rather than on independent research?

1201. What were the most significant issues on this Policy Management Tools project?

1202. Did the team work well together?

1203. How useful was the format and content of the Policy Management Tools project Status Report to you?

1204. How effective was each Policy Management Tools project Team member in fulfilling his/her role?

1205. Who is responsible for each action?

1206. Did the Policy Management Tools project improve the team members reputations, skills, personal development?

Index

permission   1
person 1, 22, 163, 182, 194
personal   265
personally   147
personnel   18, 25, 62, 97, 140, 154, 166, 176
pertinent   97
phases 55, 89, 200, 242, 263
pitfalls 107
placed229
places 181
planet 102
planned   92, 94, 96, 101, 143, 154, 157, 198, 203-204, 262
planners   93
planning   3, 9, 97, 101, 130, 136, 138, 140, 142, 154, 165,
167, 222, 230, 246, 256
platform   239
platforms   238
players82
pocket174
pockets   174
points 27, 43, 58, 65, 74, 91, 103, 127, 134
policies   139, 250-251
policing   250
Policy 1-6, 8-14, 16-43, 45-58, 60-117, 119-144, 146, 148-152,
154-155, 157-161, 163, 165, 167, 169-172, 174-181, 183, 185-189,
191, 193, 195-209, 211-213, 215-217, 219-223, 225-227, 229, 231-
236, 238, 240-252, 254-265
political   119, 134, 200, 205
population   137
portfolio   243
portfolios   240
portray62
position   195
positioned   183-184
positive   84, 105, 119, 150, 217
possess245
possible   49, 60, 64, 79, 92, 117, 121, 175, 220, 230, 251,
259
post-test   238
potential   25, 55, 73, 77-78, 83, 91, 106, 126, 155, 193, 206,
235
practical   71, 75, 79, 92, 221-222
practice   208

resolve 16, 21, 237
resolved   130, 177, 241
resource   3-4, 121, 140, 143, 167, 169, 171, 197, 212, 222
resources   2, 8, 22-24, 29, 37, 41, 56, 60, 86, 98, 100, 114,
121, 138, 140, 154, 158, 161-162, 166, 169, 172, 176, 179, 183,
185, 187, 198, 212, 216, 235-236, 245
respect   1
respond   203
responded   12
response   22, 25, 92-94, 102-103, 253
responses   119, 203
responsive   183
result   82, 84, 137, 149, 183, 186, 188-189, 218, 225, 230, 236,
260, 262
resulted   97
resulting   61, 198
results 9, 32, 40, 64, 75-76, 79-81, 84-88, 94-95, 136-137, 140,
155, 176, 184, 230, 239, 254
Retain 104
retained   67, 197
retention   57
retrospect   120
return 84, 109
revenue   23
revenues   53
review 10, 41, 72, 131, 165, 176-177, 182, 186, 204, 211, 227, 230,
234, 238
reviewed   34, 151, 158, 216
reviewers   237
reviews155, 211, 238
revised 67, 97, 154
revisions   261
revisit 228
reward 51, 54, 72, 221
rewarded   24
rewards   100
rework 51, 54
rights   1
robustness   164
roll-out 217
routine 97, 246
safety 111
samples   188

299

CPSIA information can be obtained
at www.ICGtesting.com
Printed in the USA
BVHW041010200819
556236BV00011B/674/P

9 780655 841685